How to Eat a Pizza From a Can:

Volume IV of The Travels of Senator & Wendy V

- © 2011 by Wendy V. All rights reserved. No part of this publication may be reproduced or transmitted in any form or by any means, electronic or mechanical, including photocopy, recording, or any information storage and retrieval system, without the prior written consent of the author and/or publisher.

- cover photography © 2011 by David Zuchowski.

ISBN: 978-0-99150-933-1

for Senator—

Why don't you slip into something more comfortable before reading this?

"Not all those who wander are lost."

~J. R. R. Tolkien

Table of Contents

Introduction	i.
Facation	1
Light My Lamp	9
My Grandma and My Dali	27
Door #2	59
Victorian Mosquitoes	85
No Kinda' Ground	105
Bonus!	133
Do You Know the Way to San José? How About I-5, Then?	139
Afterword	165

Author's Note

See Author's Note, *How to Read a Compass in the Dark*. Better yet, just buy the first three books in this series.

Introduction

Grandma asked again. Lately it seems that every phone conversation we have eventually rolls around to that familiar question, casually and stealthily worked in. "Have you been writing lately, Honey?" She knows! I am afraid to disappoint-- her or myself. Let the torrent of excuses begin. I've been working a lot. (True, but lame.) I'm getting ready to write. (Sure, if by getting ready you mean strangling the nagging voice in the back of my head that is desperately trying to construct some vague sense of the first chapter.) Thus, six months after I originally meant to, I am describing the events that comprise the fourth two-year cycle of our travels. For always asking and encouraging, I thank you, Grandma.

I must confess I am apprehensive about the quantity of material with which I have to work. It seems like during the first few years we were jetting off to new experiences every few months. Now, mainly due to the acquisition of my 'big-girl job', escaping together requires strategic planning, and significant patience during the interim of dry spells. As anyone who has taught school recently will tell you, long, lazy summers off are a myth. Still, we managed to cover some more territory in the beautiful and diverse United States of America, revisiting familiar trails and exploring new ones. So stick out your thumb and we'll bring you along for the ride.

~Wendy V
January 2010

Chapter 1
Facation:
Summer 2009

Fa-ca-tion *(fay-KAY'-shun)* n. 1.a period of multiple consecutive days free from one's employer, often involving leaving one's residence, suggesting fun and relaxation, however in reality yielding dividends ranging from minor inconvenience to pain and financial loss 2.any excursion where the work factor far outweighs the fun factor 3.similar to a vacation, only completely different.

June 1st Senator and I celebrated the six best years of my life together. It had been a busy spring, filled with new challenges. Senator continued to experiment with his mobile production gear by recording friends' local bands.* It has been an ongoing learning curve, and there are always new aspects of the

---

* At one point in late February, one such adventure found me sitting alone in an ugly, depressing country dive bar that had seen neither a decorating update nor a fresh pot of coffee since the late 1970s, as evidenced by the glittering hula hoops on the wall and the indoor wooden Shaker shingles. Senator was busy speeding the hour-long trip back home to retrieve a forgotten cable, while I sat, simultaneously disturbed and mesmerized by Teddy, the ugly and cocky pedal steel player with the pompadour straight out of Eastern Tennessee.

technology to learn, few of which could be described as fun. Intermittently, the summer and following seasons had been devoted to this.

My challenges were not as cerebral, but of a more physical nature. In late May I was informed that I had an intruding pea in my boob. Actually, that's my paraphrase, although that is the best description I could think of. Like I just swallowed a veggie wrongly one day and there landed the offending legume, completely misguided en route to my stomach.

The actual diagnosis rejected the pea theory in exchange for something along the lines of a 'fibro adenoma tumor within the breast tissue'. I liked mine better. I remember thinking that this was the part where I was supposed to be scared. Then I was supposed to watch daytime television chick shows to feel inspired by some sappy celebrity 'survivor' who would uphold me in the Battle of the Boob.

Whoa. Back up the train. I knew the odds of it being cancer were slim, especially given my lifestyle, but I couldn't help being angry. *What impudence!* I had it out with my body. *How dare you? I take damn good care of you every day-- with the exception of a fine pizza now and then but nobody's perfect-- and this is how you treat me?*

Needless to say I did not take the suggestion of surgery well. Surgery? Me? The only time I had experienced something similar was when I was eighteen and I had my wisdom teeth out. I had generally repressed the memory, but I do not recall it as a banner day in my life. It was not the pain that bothered me so much as the idea of losing consciousness. Basically, I am the opposite of Michael Jackson. I will do anything to *avoid* anesthetics. Call me a control freak, but I like being able to move my own body and think coherent thoughts as an aware member of the human race.

After examining all options, Senator and I determined

that the surgery was in my best interest. I tried to bargain with the doctor, promising him that I would lie very still and not say a word if he would just let me get by with a tiny amount of local anesthetic. He actually laughed in my face. "You know, most people like the idea of not seeing or feeling anything." It was obvious he did not know Wendy V.

In mid-June the big day arrived. I had been downing twenty or more cherries each day in anticipation of a speedy recovery. I had read somewhere that they inhibited pain transmission, and I would only have the weekend to recover and get my act together before returning to my summer school teaching assignment. As an added precaution, for the thirty-six hours leading up to the surgery I had consumed only liquids. *If I kick the bucket on the operating table, at least it won't be because I choked on my own vomit. That would be awful, no matter how rock star it is.*

Senator was with me until the last possible moment. He was there when the nurse took all of my vital signs. (*Woo-hoo! Lost two pounds!*) He was there when I got the i.v., holding my hand as I had bad flashbacks to an excruciating experience involving an i.v. when I was in high school. I still remember my frozen gaze at his shirt zipper as I put myself into a needle-coping trance. The poor nurse kept asking if I was alright, but I knew if I spoke, my concentration would be broken and I would be a mess. He explained on my behalf. "She's fine. Just do your thing." He was even there for me when my anesthesiologist introduced himself. *Did he just say his name was "Dr. Kavorkian"? Oh, Kavori. Got it. That's better.*

In the end my stubborn mental demand for wellness paid off. The surgery went shockingly fast and was a grand success. Afterward I was given a strong prescription for pain medication, but I never felt so much as mild discomfort. Monday morning I was back at work, my ugly but temporary Frankenboob incision known only to me. All was good again, but this was just the beginning of summer facation.

In the weeks that followed, we enjoyed less eventful days. We found a new secluded bike trail to enjoy-- the kind where you pass more animals than people. Then my sister came for a weekend, which always includes plenty of laughter. In fact, June went out on a quiet and serene note, and now we were looking forward to a real vacation in July.

Our good friends Bill and Marge had once again invited us to join them in Door County, Wisconsin, for a few days of bike riding, relaxing, and visiting by the campfire.* Senator and I were more than ready for a break, and we counted down the days until we could run away together. However, with just two days to go before leaving, we received the news that our friend's mother had passed away. We canceled our plans so we could be with him and attend the arrangements. I couldn't help but wonder if our old pattern of pre-vacation misfortune was returning.

The wake and funeral fell in the middle of a four day stretch that Senator had taken off, leaving him some extra time to work with the upgraded recording software he had purchased. The new acquisition violated his vow to himself that, once he had all components of digital recording functioning properly, he would never be lured into more complex systems and, consequently more problems/glitches/headaches by a seductive upgraded version. But the road to computer hell is paved, maintained, and signed by good intentions.

In a yuppie bar in Naperville, surrounded by too many tables and far too many desperate, drunk, 40-something white women who thought they could sing... and dance... and look significantly better than they did, the computer crashed. Rows of the pretty dancing lights that indicate successful input of data fell dark for a few moments. While this is not such a big deal

---

* See *How to Start a Fire Under the Sea*

when you are recording the pop standards cover band of a friend-of-a-friend for free, it was sure to put a damper on the following weeks' assignment to record a world-class jazz trio. Yay technology.

Hours of tech support phone calls, emails, and research led to the decision to scrap the current hardware and buy a beast of a system that would effortlessly record entire orchestras conducted underwater at unprecedented sampling rates, if that is what the producer so desired. The commitment was made, and the reluctant checkbook creaked open again. As time was of the essence, we decided to forgo the shipping and drive to pick up the new baby in person. So far facation had kept us from Wisconsin, but by golly on a Monday morning at 7:00am we were on our way to sunny Fort Wayne, Indiana.

Arriving at Sweetwater, 'the world's leading music technology and instrument retailer', was surreal. We stretched our legs after the three hour and forty-five minute drive. A large, open, tastefully decorated gallery surrounded the information desk, where receptionists in headsets paged sales representatives to court customers and their retail dollars. The facility was beautiful and overwhelming. While waiting for the service technicians to install the software, our personal sales rep gave us the tour.

We visited the state-of-the-art studios and the theatres where training seminars were held. As we sipped our bitter leading-music-retailer coffee, he showed us the racquetball court and hair salon that the employees enjoyed. *Do they ever let you leave?* we wanted to ask, but thought better of it. Finally, he led us to the ping pong tables and virtual golf pad so we could wait with the other customers who, I could only assume, were on facation as well.

Soon the new computer was snuggled into the back seat for the ride home. If there was anything of note between Forte Wayne, Indiana, and La Salle County, Illinois, I missed it. I did, however, take it as a good omen when we passed an old barn bearing the name 'Vandermark Farms'. Vandermark, coincidentally, was the name of the saxophone player who headed up the trio that Senator was preparing to record.

It was mid-July and summer was cruising swiftly along. With three days off in the middle of the week, we packed the recording gear for gigs in Chicago and Milwaukee. Ever the realist, I informed my travel companion that we could drive home Wednesday night after the Chicago performance, but there was no way we were going to drive the three hours home the next night after the Milwaukee concert. Besides, if we got a hotel, we could make a night of it and pretend we weren't there to work, right?

The Chicago show went as planned, and Senator even relaxed a bit during the second set. One down, one to go. The next morning we slept in and repacked the equipment for Milwaukee. Traffic cooperated nicely and we found our hotel easily. Of course, the problem wasn't in finding the hotel, but in finding a way into the hotel. One-way streets and a hidden parking deck conspired to drive us in circles a few times before we could crack the code. Actually, the whole institution was a labyrinth.

Once we checked in, we could not find the elevators without exploring numerous nooks and secluded corners. Likewise, what should have been a simple exit to an outdoor courtyard led to the inside of a mall. Perhaps this was some deranged tourism strategy. "Milwaukee-- Good luck getting out!"

Milwaukee has also made the grave mistake of following big brother Chicago into the den of outsourced parking meters. It's a great system, provided you do not mind paying four times too much to park, walking a few blocks to find a pay box, wondering if you are being ticketed during your walk to said pay box, and fighting with the pay box to accept payment while trying not to advertise the fact that you, unarmed, are using a valid credit card.

Nevertheless, the evening at The Sugar Maple went well. Hamid Drake (percussion), Kent Kessler (bass), and Ken Vandermark (reeds), wowed the packed crowd with a rare DKV Trio performance of their integrated free jazz. All uniquely improved pieces were captured for historical purposes on... an old digital recorder that Senator had brought along when he realized, in untold frustration, that the new computer was refusing to play nicely. While he was able to obtain a solid, workable recording, he was back to square one on the hardware front. Don't get me wrong, Reader. It has always been a dream of ours to see Fort Wayne together, walking hand-in-hand through a large parking lot that borders the romantic cornfields of Indiana, but wasted time is always bitter.

The next morning we checked out of the maze hotel and rewarded ourselves for finding the front desk by going to breakfast. The hotel buffet was not spectacular, but reasonably pleasant. I was particularly intrigued by the waffle maker. This little miracle of science allows the waffle makee to, as demonstrated by the buffet attendant, dump a 2/3 full Dixie cup of batter on it, lock down the handles, set the timer, rotate at the appropriate ding, and produce the perfect waffle. Or so goes the story.

Apparently I had not learned my lesson about the way our summer was becoming inextricably intertwined with the perils of technology. Even after following directions precisely, the Wendy waffle was a dripping mess of raw batter overrunning charred and encrusted residue, and now rapidly beginning to smoke. I did my best to hide the evidence and unrotate the 360° culinary disaster.* I tried hard to ignore the child who looked at me in disbelief and disgust. At any moment I expected her to summon her mommy, the buffet attendant, or the house detective.†

We finished our breakfast and walked out to the car in the parking deck. Senator had recorded two nights in a row, but it felt like we had been gone a week. The ride home was a peaceful change of pace from cities and crowded venues and blaring saxophones. We made a point to recognize this, especially since it would be 'back to the drawing board' when Senator got home. It was still man vs. machine, and man (and the woman behind him) was fighting an uphill battle.

At least it appeared that facation was drawing to a close. We were finally going to sneak a real trip into the two weeks I had left before going back to school. My sister, also a teacher, was off work, and we planned to take a four day weekend to see her. On past trips to see her we had felt rushed, so I looked forward to an extra day of relaxation and time to visit. There would be no work involved, and the only agenda was a fun afternoon kayaking on a calm lake. With a few days to go before this trip, however, the Summer of All Things Defective reared its ugly head once more.

---

* Incidentally, the little drip tray beneath buffet liquids is just that-- a *little* drip tray. For larger spills, I recommend a subtle handful of 12-15 napkins, swiped casually over the area, while a trusted associate creates a diversion.

† I'm not sure if there are house detectives anymore, but they were certainly a prolific industry according to the many old movies we watch. Their duties seemed to consist of 1.) chasing rapscallions who abused room service without paying, 2.) demanding marriage licenses of couples with suspiciously little luggage, and 3.) fast-walking through lobbies with stern looks on their faces just before slipping on banana peels, allowing the stowaway guests to make a run for it.

Chapter 2
Light My Lamp:
Early August 2009

Thursday I took my time packing. I always savor the luxury of a day off before a trip. This is a phenomenon that only occurs if we travel in summer, and I celebrate by calmly assembling the necessary items, giving the house a good tidy, and taking a nap, satisfied in the knowledge that all is done in a timely manner. All in all, it is the ideal way to prepare for a trip.

It was early evening and I strolled downstairs to the clutter hole we call our 'office' to see what Senator was up to. "Hey, what's going on?" I asked casually. I looked down at Senator from the sixth step, my usual perch for chatting and philosophizing and dreaming about where to place the walls when we finish the basement. He didn't respond. I assumed he was absorbed in a music review or other related research. Then he began.

"Unbelievable!"

"What's that?" I was afraid to ask. Then I thought he must have just read something incredible.

"I think we have a virus, and this one's bad. I can't get out of it." Of *course* we had a virus on our computer. Why not? After all, our home computer, which we use for work, play, communication, research, and general record keeping had been all too cooperative during the various studio computer meltdowns. Apparently it now demanded its turn at disrupting our lives and causing us to lose long strands of hair.

This particular virus was a beast. It did not come through a bogus email scam, but popped up as, ironically, a warning against a potential virus. It then offered to run a scan, which, if performed, would dig you deeper into the hole. Eventually, if you followed it all the way through, I imagine it would have asked for a credit card number, pretending to sell you protection. Though we never made it that far, we were stuck nonetheless. This sucker was not going away, and we had no idea what files might be lost or damaged. Ggrrr!

When our attempts at fixing the monster failed, Senator placed a few phone calls to our network of acquaintances who know more about computers than we do, which pretty much consists of everyone under the age of fifty. Thankfully, my brother Jason responded. He had a plan to fix it that, if successful, would only take him a few hours. It was too late to have him come over that night, so we agreed to cut our trip short by a day and take care of it then.

Leaving town with a problem still hanging over your head is never ideal, but maybe that's when we most need vacations. My parents have had this experience a few times, thanks to poor timing on the part of various appliances and sections of plumbing. My mother's attitude is that, as long as you can do nothing about it, you may as well not worry about it, either. Good advice, Mom. We did our best to follow it. So, we were downsized to a three day run to Springfield, Missouri and back.

I love going to see my sister, but I do not love *going* to see my sister. Though I appreciate any time Senator and I have uninterrupted hours to talk, there are other routes I would much rather drive. For starters, Illinois is just boring. Once you have seen ten minutes on the interstate, you have pretty much taken in the entire variety of landscape. We got corn. Near the Missouri border, for about four seconds, it is exciting to see the St. Louis Arch, until you remember that it means you will soon be fighting for your spot when six lanes converge into two.

Once in Missouri, defensive driving is the official state sport. It wouldn't be so bad if you just had to deal with aggressive drivers. We would know what to do; Chicagoland breeds them. Instead, you must deal with unpredictable drivers, which gets tiresome very fast. Like to brake while going uphill? Why not? Have trouble choosing a lane? Just hang out in the center for awhile. Take your time, plenty of room.

Billboards in Missouri are different, too. For starters, there are only two kinds: tourism and religion. Whether your destiny be Branson or Heaven, you can be sure a giant road sign will be there to guide you, often from hundreds of miles away. We passed one billboard that simply read "Jesus". I'm not sure how I feel about that. I assume the renter wanted to give a message of hope and peace, but does Christ belong on a marketing tool that just last week beckoned disciples of the local casino?

Sooner than expected, we were happy to arrive in Springfield. We did not go directly to my sister's home, but instead checked into a hotel. Heidi, in her endless efforts to maintain a social life that would keep five people busy, had another guest that evening. Her close friend and former roommate was in town and needed a place to crash en route from Texas to Illinois. Edith is a fun and pleasant girl, but visions of the four of us clamoring over each other to share a bathroom and limited floor space suggested that a hotel was the best solution for Senator and me.

We pulled up to the Lamplighter Inn, which had been recommended by my parents, who had stayed there when Heidi was still living in a college dorm. Naturally, we had a good chuckle over the name. Where we come from, the only thing named "Lamplighter" is a strip joint about ten miles away. This establishment was decidedly different. At least I assumed so, since the logo did not have silhouettes of skinny, long-haired girls dancing around poles.

We settled into the G-rated Lamplighter, and in ten minutes Senator was asleep. It's strange how driving can exhaust a person. I phoned Heidi to let her know we were in town, and that we would be over in about an hour. It was great to hear her voice and know that I would see her soon. As I hung up the phone, I noticed the wall jack for a computer, which made me think of the virus mess that awaited us back home. So far, we had done well ignoring it, but I thought I had better crawl in next to Senator for a relaxing nap, just in case.

Before long we were awakened by the high-pitched beeps of the alarm clock. It took a second to realize where I was. *Oh right-- the 'other' Lamplighter.* Time to dance over to Heidi's place.

Soon we arrived at the apartment to the giggles and smiles of my sister and her friend. I was reminded of a week six years earlier, when I was their temporary guest at their apartment back in Joliet. For reasons beyond my control, I was homeless for one month, despite the fact that I owned a home. Heidi and Edith graciously gave me the rights to their couch, in return for which I had to provide them with all of the juicy details about the mysterious character known only as 'Senator', who took an hour and a half to say goodnight at the front door. I will never forget their kindness, or Edith's declaration that she needed to get herself a senator, too. I agree; every girl should have one.

The four of us joked and traded stories and laughed our way to a nearby Indian restaurant. Though none of us were drinking, the restaurant staff must have thought we were all sloshed because we were a compounded pile of silly. It only got worse when we dropped one of the boxes of leftovers in the parking lot. A piece of Indian fennel bread spun out onto the blacktop. There were no garbage cans around, and it was a short trip back to Heidi's, so we brought it along with us.

When we got back to the apartment, Senator made a detour to where our truck was parked and deposited the soiled leftovers into the bed. I tried to protest, but I couldn't get the words out because I was laughing too hard. "That's the stupidest... Birds don't eat Indian... *Now* who looks like the hillbillies?" I sputtered out. The thought of local birds discussing the strange find was completely hilarious to me.

Hey there, Blue. What d'ya make of this crazy lookin' bread?

No idear, Robin. T'aint Wonder Bread-- that's fer sure. I notice there's some kinda seeds in there, too.

Oh yeah. I see 'em. Must be they're makin' birdseed fer lazy folks now. Instead of goin' out an' fillin' up our feeders, they just have ta throw these here round things out like frisbees.

Land sakes! What will those crazy humans think of next?

At Heidi's we made a quick pit stop before heading to Springfield's downtown. It was an art walk night, which meant that the surrounding blocks were alive with gallery showings, buzzing coffee houses, street musicians, college kids, and a host of other energetic souls. It had been a cooler summer in most states, making the evenings ideal for bumming around outdoors. Our objectives were simple: people watch, and at some point consume a well-roasted cup of coffee.

One thing to love about downtown Springfield is the ample parking. It is virtually hassle-free, and if there was any charge, I don't recall it. I firmly avow that, if municipalities really want to come out ahead revenue-wise, they should provide plenty of free parking to attract customers and tourists. The money gained in sales tax and the communal benefits surrounding thriving businesses would more than make up for a little bit of money lost on parking.*

We found a convenient spot next to what appeared to be an old rusted-out fire truck. This strange antique was comfortably perched upon the curbside, with little explanation. That's okay; none was needed. I assumed it was part of the local history, and the fact that I could see no local historical firehouse was a mere inconsequential detail. The four of us climbed out of the car and stretched our legs.

Walking about a block toward the action, we could see crowds of people milling about the streets. It was only a few moments before my sister ran into someone she knew. "Hey, what are *you* doing here? I was just thinking about you! I'm so glad you're here because I always wanted my sister to meet you!" Introductions followed, and a moment later I promptly forgot who the woman was.

This is a typical scene when you are out with Heidi. To date, she has roughly 1,209 close friends, and a host of acquaintances whom she regularly contacts. And they all adore her.† This is the sort of popularity to which I can not relate. Don't get me wrong, Reader; your author is a fairly easy-to-get-along-with type. I just have a small, select group of people with whom I am close. As for the rest, I know I would never keep up with them, so I don't bother. There it is-- realism in action.

I breathed in the surprisingly dry night air and squeezed Senator's hand. Moments like this still thrill me. It was enough to bum around and people watch. Street musicians added to the carefree atmosphere as well. Most were not bad, but it was

---

* Proposal based on no distinguishable data, although, one has yet to disprove my theory.

† I first realized this when I volunteered to be a chaperone on one of Heidi's high school field trips to Chicago. We were gone the entire day, and it was about once per hour that we craned our necks to see who was yelling, "Hey Heidi!" Never mind the fact that we were in a city of 3,000,000 people.

comical to hear them playing far too close to each other. It's not often one is treated to such a vibrant collage of bits and pieces of so many two-chord covers.

The four of us paused in our stride to take in a group of girls donned in plastic dresses. Maybe a bachelorette party? The colorful concoctions sported vinyl fringe and trim. They were creatively assembled, and, I'm sure, absolute torture to wear, but the girls were clearly enjoying themselves.

Not all of the patrons of downtown Springfield were so merry. Turning down another block took us past The Protesters. A handful of dour college-aged kids looked at the crowds in disgust, as they steadfastly raised their homemade signs. On the signs, random Bible verses pronounced judgment against... what? Evil pedestrians? The shameless debauchery of people strolling around on a summer night?

Whenever I see such people acting like idiots and giving Christians a bad name, I have multiple reactions, including but not limited to: 1.)amusement, 2.)a strong desire to grab one of their signs and join in, just to surprise them, 3.)pity, and 4.)the distinct vision of Christ sighing, slowly shaking his head side-to-side in his hand, saying, "Not again?! They just don't get it." It reminds me of a bumper sticker I once saw that read "Lord, save us from your people". *Amen.*

The streets were buzzing with activity now as we followed Heidi into one of many galleries that was open late for the art walk. The studio was entirely devoted to glass work. Behind a wall worked an expert glassblower, patiently shaping the syrupy colors into exquisite baubles. The entire shop was filled with hand-blown[*] jewelry, vases, and other trinkets. Edith and Heidi fingered and admired bracelets and paperweights. I

---

[*] Although, I contend that the term 'mouth-blown' would be more accurate. Alas, the name Wendy V has yet to earn respect in the glass art community.

knew better, though. I wasn't about to press my luck around so many breakables. While I am an average dancer who can shake it well enough to good music, and I can balance a heavy service tray high over my shoulder, I am not known for my grace when performing simple motor skills, like walking past a filled display case. I thought it best not to tempt fate.

We wandered around some more, ducking in and out of galleries that caught our interest. Heidi particularly studied the photography exhibits. I, of course, declared that my little sister could out-pose and out-shoot any of them. Her talent in this area has excelled, and I fully expect to see her work displayed in one of these galleries someday... unless they're too afraid of the competition!

Soon our meanderings took the inevitable detour into one of Springfield's many coffee houses. It smelled rich and warm and wonderful, and we took the long line of the eager precaffeinated twenty-somethings as a good sign. Apparently this place had a reputation that gave people good reason to wait. According to the International Coffee Organization[*], North Americans have been brewin' the bean since 1668. I surmised that the person in the front of the line, who was currently being served, first entered the coffee shop during roughly that time. Service was s..........l..........o..........w. But that was okay. As I have expounded upon in a previous book, vacation time allows one to experience, and yes, even embrace, a pace that he/she would otherwise find infuriating. Here, the wait only served to enhance the anticipation.

Of course, the problem with enhanced anticipation, no matter how romantic the author has described the setting, is that it builds you up for a grand letdown when it doesn't deliver. *Sigh.* I took the entire wait time to decide on the perfect latte

---

[*] Visit www.ico.org for more information on the history of the American love affair with coffee.

combination. Caramel, vanilla soy milk, and just a hint of white chocolate over a conservative amount of ice was presented as I plunked down the cash. Senator opted for straight java offset by a gooey confection. I twirled my straw around to spin the ice in the cup and maximize the flavor.

As we stepped outside, I took my first sip. *Hhmmm, not quite what I expected.* I tried another. Boooo. They forgot the caramel and white chocolate. Worse yet, they skimped on the coffee. Double boooo. My beverage was instantly reduced to a glorified soy milk on the rocks. That's what I get for splurging. Had I just ordered my standard black coffee, there would not have been any other ingredients to forget. As guilty as I feel about wasting, I slowly dumped it along the street.

Senator then diverted my attention. He pointed out the town square breakdancers. A group was forming around three guys doing their best to keep 1982 alive and spinning. Hands, shoulders, and heads all served as platforms for the characteristic rotating, hopping, and robotic movements. I have to say, they were quite good.

Across the way, another dying art form prevailed. The local mime[*] imitated unwary individuals. Soon he was predictably trapped in an invisible box. *Good, maybe he'll stay put for awhile.* Right on cue, however, he magically escaped in time to direct a truck that was backing up. The best part was watching him 'yell' silently to the driver to turn his wheel. Now this I can appreciate, for the pure uselessness of it. Observing futility from the outside can be satisfying. Amazingly, the truck backed through the crowd without injuring anyone. At least, I don't think anyone was hurt. Anyone heard from the mime lately?...

Our trek through Springfield's downtown took us through and around many blocks, killing much of the evening.

---

[*] Every town should have one.

We agreed that it was time to head back, so the four of us left the energy of the downtown for the quiet of a dark side street. We piled into Heidi's car for the 50¢ tour on the way back to her apartment. Sitting down in the back seat, I suddenly realized how tired I was. I looked over at Senator, who was still alert, but within an hour of feeling as exhausted as I was.

The culmination of the tour of places-associated-with-Heidi's-transplanted-life culminated with Fun Acres. You guessed it. The name says it all. There are batting cages, mini-golf courses, and dozens of gleeful customers enjoying every inch of the ¼ acre or so that comprises Fun Acres. (Though inaccurate, I guess leaving the plural 's' off the name would have made it seem too piteous.)

Through choked laughter, Heidi told us about goofing off at Fun Acres with her friends from college. It had become a local joke with them, a guaranteed laugh at parties. After all, how could anyone sustain a sullen mood with a name like that? She pulled into a parking space momentarily so we could view the Fun firsthand. It was then that we looked over to the right and exploded into hysterics. For this, we are forever four rotten individuals.

In the minivan next to us, gazing longingly out of the back seat window, was a young boy of about eight or nine years old. No one else was in the van, which made the hoards of Fun Acres patrons all the more painful to watch. I could only imagine the family conversation that spawned this pathetic scene:

"If I told you once, I told you a thousand times-- leave your sister alone or you'll be sorry!"

"But she was on *my* side of the back seat!"

"Knock it off or I'll turn this car right around and no one will have any Fun!"

[*dramatic girlish sobbing*] "Daaaaaaad! He just did it agaaaaaaaiiiiiiin!"

"That's it! Enough is enough. Oh, we're still going to Fun Acres-- don't you worry-- but your mother and I will take your sister in and you can just wait here!"

[*dramatic boyish sobbing*] "Nooooooo!"

"Daddy, can I have his popcorn money?..."

The taunting shadow of the gleaming electric Fun Acres sign fell ironically on the lad. Now tell me you would have been able to hold a straight face either, Reader.

Shortly after, we returned to Heidi's place. We recapped a few of the evening's highlights and said our goodbyes. Edith was staying. We were heading back to the Lamplighter, clothing intact.

Walking through the stale smelling lobby of the hotel reminded me that some states still do not demonize indoor smoking. We hurried along to the stairs and clomped up to our room. Moments later we were performing our nightly routine of brushing our teeth while walking around.* Despite the uneasy quiet of a foreign bed, we fell asleep instantly.

Saturday morning was ripe for adventure. Senator dozed a few extra minutes while I got ready. This left me with a surplus of time to kill while he took a shower. *Let's see what's on the idiot box.* I turned on the Weather Channel to get my groove on. I shimmied my way through the five day forecast, and two-stepped past the humidity reading. August in Missouri could be hazardous to this cold-blooded girl's health, but we would be on a lake, hopefully contained within a kayak.

When the Weather Channel's jazz faded, I switched to my other hotel room cable obsession: the Travel Channel, of course.

---

*I don't remember how this started, but for some reason, Senator and I roam around while brushing. We rarely stay put over the sink. After a couple of minutes of dancing around the house, I usually end up racing back to the sink, hand under chin, attractively resembling a rabid chipmunk. Senator, on the other hand, could go for hours. The boy can hold his toothpaste.

It was one of those road shows that tours the U.S. of A. in search of the greatest manifestations of one particular food. The subject of the day's homage was the doughnut (or donut, if you prefer). While you may have thought you were getting wild the last time you enjoyed an apple cinnamon or frosted raspberry jelly variety, the experience will pale by comparison to such delights as the grape doughnut. No, not grape flavored, but grape. Very retro looking. Half-orbs of glossy green or purple resting like bubbles on a traditional ring. Or maybe you can't give up your kid cereal addiction. Then sample a doughnut covered in Froot Loops. Never been able to fit into the round peg of life? Try a square doughnut instead. Go ahead. Rock your world. Possibly the two most interesting were the Heart Attack Special[*], which incorporated fried bacon on top of the fried dough (no charge for the extra grease), and the voodoo doughnut, complete with inserted pretzel sticks.

We packed our bag and checked out. Driving to Heidi's seemed to take longer than it should have. It could be because, unless you are taking an obscure road through a neighborhood in Springfield, you will encounter about forty-eight stoplights per mile of travel. As you are patiently (or not) sitting at one, dozens more taunt you as you look ahead to the endless line of hurdles. Moving to the middle of nowhere has spoiled me quickly. It didn't take long to get used to driving for thirty minutes at a time uninterrupted.

Heidi was still getting ready when we arrived. She and Edith had stayed up late catching up during their brief window of time together. Senator and I kicked back on Heidi's futon/couch. On the television, a scientist was discussing Einstein's theories involving the space-time continuum. You would think one of us would get the remote and change the channel, but we didn't. It was so over our heads that it was

---

[*] Not actual name.

strangely compelling. Perhaps it was the juxtaposition of being on vacation while processing hard academics. Perhaps Heidi's home just lent itself to the study of astrophysics. The last time I was there I was reading Einstein's biography. I noted that the scientist on t.v. left out all of the juicy bits about his personal life. No affairs here; just straight up $E=mc^2$.

When Heidi was ready, we left for Table Rock. For months we had been anticipating a canoe or kayak trip. I had only gone canoeing once, and I had never been in a kayak. Senator had never done either. When she called for information, Heidi learned that kayaks were available, and they could hold three people.

This made me feel better. The only kayaks I had ever seen were the ones on television, where an individual is encased in the skinny contraption up to his waist. When not perfectly balanced, he flips upside down, and, if it was me, drowns. Not so with these kayaks. The New Zealander who owned the shop showed us the vessel, which was basically a low-slung plastic canoe. "We'll take it!"

We drove to the beach and the Kiwi dropped off our kayak and life jackets. "Kell me if yew wunt me to cam back airly. Ootherwise, E'll see yew in tew arrs." We clumsily fitted our life jackets on, noting the distinct odor of equipment that has been used by many other people in similar wet circumstances.

Three people, three aligned seats. Who goes where? We unanimously voted Senator to the rear for leg space and anchoring. Heidi seemed to be in captain mode, so she took front, leaving me in the middle. Everybody carefully found her or his or her spot and settled in. No tips so far. We were pretty good.

We shoved off into shallow water and stroked our double-sided paddles in unison. The Viking ships had nothing on us. Senator should have brought a drum. Smooth as silk, until... *slap, splosh, slap, splosh, slap slap, splosh splosh.*

As it turned out, we were not as tight as we thought. Senator had a productive rhythm going, but Heidi paddled at a more casual pace. I, stuck in the middle, could only match one at a time without smacking paddles or injuring myself. I naturally tended to match Senator, which probably has something to do with our mutual accomplishment/conqueror-prone personalities.[*] At times I would make a conscious effort to match Heidi. At other times I would give up and only use one paddle, which seemed to minimize the effects. Somehow our syncopation propelled us a mile away, still without any spills.

We made it to the closest island out in the lake. Other shores in the distance had large homes and boathouses, but this island was small and deserted. We pulled the kayak onto the sandy beach, making sure it could not float off and leave us stranded. While it might have made my story better, we had already dealt with enough mishaps over the summer. At least no computer was involved in this excursion.

We stretched our legs on the beach and viewed the region. Hhmmm. It's kind of funny how the landscape looks very different when you are facing the route back. We surveyed our options. I was pretty sure we came from *that* inlet, but Senator said it was one over to the right. Heidi voted for left. At least we all agreed that we needed to go back in the general direction from which we came.

We lingered a little while longer before climbing back into the kayak. I was the first one in, and Heidi followed. As Senator was getting in, I tried to brace the wrong way and we tipped the sucker over. That figures. Go all the way there without incident and capsize in fourteen inches of water. Good thing we were wearing our life vests.

We never did get our three person paddling rhythm

---

[*] I'm sure a psychologist could have fun with that, but I'm not paying $120 per hour.

down, but the trip back was wonderful. My only tense moment was when I saw a smallish (but still too big for me) snake slithering on the water's surface about ten feet from our boat. Thankfully, he paid no attention to us before moving on. I don't mind little snakes scurrying away from me on a trail, but a kayak sits very low into the water, and I would hate to think of that creature suddenly floating over the side into my lap. They would have heard me screaming back in Illinois!

Closer to the shoreline, it became apparent which nook we needed to seek. We beached our kayak and unhooked the life jackets. More families were approaching, many of them clumsier than us, which made me feel good about our first attempt at kayaking. Soon the Kiwi returned. "Ho'd yew lak et? Yew ken go oot agen far a few mur arrs ef yew lak..."

"We had a wonderful time, but thanks, I think we'll have to get back now," I answered. The sun, the wind, and the upper body workout had tired us. Now our focus was on another great regional favorite-- Lambert's.

Lambert's requires preparation. One cannot just race willy-nilly to the onslaught of exaggerated Southern portions. We first went to Heidi's to clean up, dry up, and rest up. I have noticed that choosing not to have a television in one's home makes everyone else's t.v. viewing habits fascinating. Heidi, one of the most profoundly gentle and innocent creatures I know, happens to relish any good documentary starring cadavers or potential victims. Thus, Shark Week on the Discovery Channel[*] was a natural choice for the afternoon's entertainment.

The part that always gets me are the interviews with the

---

[*] As far as my research concludes, every week on the Discovery Channel falls into the topical category of either sharks, dinosaurs, or ancient mysteries. I was not particularly shocked to learn that 2009 marked the 22nd annual Shark Week, featuring all new casualties. Have people learned nothing about their potential role as bait in the food chain?

loved ones of those who have lost battles with sharks. How does a journalist approach this horrible topic? "Hello, my name is John and I'm from the Discovery Channel. As you may know, Shark Week 2009 (over 29 million viewers last year!) is right around the corner and it's never too early to stir up public panic as the masses head to the coasts on summer vacation. I understand your son was viciously maimed and died a slow, excruciating death in the jaws of a shark while showing his beautiful fiancé his latest surfing techniques. I'm hoping we could film an interview? I'll pop for the coffee..."

I guess when you have successfully produced two decades' worth of Shark Weeks, you can sneak meaningless statistics into the report. These facts demand further investigation, though. For instance, I learned that there were 125 unprovoked shark attacks last year. Naturally this led me to wonder how many *provoked* shark attacks had occurred. "Hey loser! Your momma was my momma's handbag! I eat elegantly prepared seafood like you for dinner!"

I also learned that most attacks happen close to the shore, in shallow water. That couldn't have anything to do with the fact that generally humans do not travel fifty miles off the coast to swim or surf, could it? By that statistic, you would be far safer dog paddling around the middle of the Atlantic than hanging near the land. Good advice. Just have the next transcontinental cruise ship drop you off.

Just when I thought I could not take another moment of Shark Week, it was time to leave. We drove to Lambert's and added our name to the growing waiting list. On the porch out front, dozens of people in all shapes and sizes waited for their chance to partake of giant entrees, unlimited side dishes, and a flying roll or two. In far less time than expected,[*] we were seated.

---

[*] I told you my sister knows everybody.

The typical theme restaurant does not usually incorporate vegetarian options, so we always skip straight to the salad page of the menu. At Lambert's this is a treat since a typical salad might include lettuce, tomatoes, cucumbers, mushrooms, black olives, peppers, eggs, cheese, and croutons, served in a large bread bowl. In other words, we beat the system, enjoying a full meal. While we were satisfied though, our server was not. "You just want salad?!" He was incredulous. Servers often question a meatless order, but our waiter asked the funniest, simplest question I have ever heard directed at our vegetarianism. "Why?" he asked sincerely. I think we really threw him off, poor kid.

Senator, Heidi, and I ate our way to the halfway point of our dinners and then gave up. We each caught one more soaring roll[*] for tradition's sake. The natives slather it with butter and sweet sorghum. No heart healthy olive oil here, nosiree, so your best bet is to do as my grandfather does, and bless the food asking God to remove any impurities. (Although, don't be surprised if, after doing so, your food disappears completely.)

We waddled out of Lambert's and into Heidi's car. The drive to her home produced no James River sharks, thankfully. The rest of the evening was just as uneventful-- just the way I like it when we are pressed for time. We enjoyed Heidi's company and her endless tales of the crazy antics of her second graders. (At press time, they were highly disturbed that she was not married.)

The clock ticked away, and we started to get sleepy. Senator dropped onto the air mattress and fell asleep instantly. I took a little longer. Finally, I drifted off, randomly wondering if we would spend the next evening computer shopping against our will.

Around 2:00am I awoke to the strange sensation of being

---

* See *How to Start a Fire Under the Sea*

swallowed while banging my arm against the hard floor. Sharks?! No, actually it was more as if I was a hot dog surrounded by a plastic bun. *Oh, crap.* The air mattress had a hole and we were sinking fast. I woke up Senator, who was not troubled by our soggy bed in the least. We could not locate the hole, so we scooped up the pillows and blankets and heaved the pile onto the couch, conforming our limbs to maximize the space for two adults.

The next morning the sun shone in on the sad, deflated mat on the floor. It had served guests for the last time. We were stiff and anxious to get back to our own bed that night, but it was a funny sight. Heidi made it about six steps out of her bedroom before seeing the dead mattress and laughing hysterically. She tried to apologize in between chortles.

Having lain the air mattress to rest, we packed up our Trucky and followed Heidi to a local breakfast joint for a final meal together. In just one month she would be coming to stay with us for my cousin's wedding. Then she would be back at Thanksgiving and Christmas. That made it a little easier to say goodbye.

We left the restaurant, and Senator declared that he was driving. That meant business. Now, the focus was on the home front. The computer crisis patiently waited for us there. A new school year was starting in two days. Senator had another recording gig in a few weeks, yet he was still engaged in digital equipment combat. Most importantly, though, we were allies in our battles.

Chapter 3
My Grandma and My Dali: Late March 2010

The fall 2009 semester was off and running. One month into it, however, my beloved Trucky was not. Of course. After all, this was the designated Year of Malfunctioning Technology, Engineering, and Innovation. When I plodded back into the house one September morning to inform Senator that my truck would not start, he had had enough. I couldn't disagree. For the past three years the thing had given more than its rightful share of problems. This was the straw that broke the chassis' back. I knew it was fruitless to argue, but I made one weak attempt at negotiation. "Could we wait until summer, when we've had a little more time to save?"

"No way! You are not going through another winter with this piece of crap! You're not safe in this thing; I worry about you." *Ah, touché. The protection angle. I hadn't counted on that.* I was instantly reduced to a dumb, googly girl forgetting my attachment to Trucky, and remembering one of the many reasons I am so attached to Senator.

Within six days we had researched several models,

agreed on the same first choice, test drove it, bargained it down, picked it up, and enjoyed a celebratory pizza. It was probably good that Trucky pissed me off one too many times; it made for an easy transfer of motor affections. I adored every aspect of my new car, and it felt like it was built especially for me. Once my maps, spare change, cds, snow brush, and sunglasses were moved in, my new home, christened Roadie, was ready to roll.

In addition to sale of Trucky, Senator further enjoyed his winter as he found himself increasingly booked for Chicago recordings of free jazz musicians. I tagged along to the shows, which were generally on Wednesday nights, and generally left me with about three hours of sleep before school the next morning. I didn't care, though. We were having fun and enjoying rare and great music. God help me if I ever become an old woman who's not willing to sacrifice a little sleep for a little excitement.

Still, when spring break rolled around, we were both ready for a lazy escape. My only concession to responsibility would be the forty pages of notes I had packed along to study. A few weeks earlier, several of us teachers were informed that we most likely would not have jobs after the current school year. With this knowledge, I immediately took action to enhance some of my credentials by registering to take a few monster state tests. When I was a kid, I studied for tests because I would never hear the end of it if I got bad grades. In college, I studied to prove myself above the pack academically and professionally. Now, I found myself studying to justify the eighty bucks apiece the tests cost. So with sunscreen, snacks, music, and a host of handwritten random political science and geography knowledge, we started the drive to Florida.

We see my grandma every year during the warmer months, when she is in Illinois. It had been four years, though, since we had gone to see her in her migratory abode. I know it sounds absurd, but I am not particularly crazy about Florida. In the late winter or early spring, however, when we have forgotten our negative connotations of heat and humidity, a subtropical climate sounds like a good idea.

The Saturday morning that we left was a clear, hopeful kind of day. There were more stars than cars visible when we left at 5:30am. We started south through Illinois, where I was delighted to learn that there is actually a town called Farmer City, (as though we need to add fuel to the rest of the country's jokes about us). I craned my neck out the window in search of bonafide farmers.

We moved on to our first pit stop at a rest area in Kentucky, where, despite the looks of some towns, I am happy to report that indoor plumbing seems to have taken. Apparently I wasn't the only one happy about this fact. In the bathroom stall next to me I could hear a merry soul loudly singing along with the piped-in Stevie Wonder. "You can feel it all o-o-o-ver..." I hoped she was not referring to her current lavatory experience, but hey, whatever works.

I have complained, (and rightly so), about the terrible Missouri drivers, and they will always hold that #1 place in my heart. After Missouri, though, I think the next five slots go to southeastern states, in varying order. Senator and I both developed headaches in response to the hyperawareness that a trip across Tennessee during spring break necessitates. Miles are spent dodging drivers who randomly switch lanes (into you if you are not paying attention), and avoiding road kill remains that no one ever bothers to pick up. Wait, scratch that. If it is fresh enough, and there is enough good meat on it, the unfortunate beast will be spirited away from the gruesome scene by some opportunistic hunter-gatherer.

Georgia drivers were only slightly better, but that was mitigated by the fact that we could see a thirty-five mile traffic jam on the opposite side of the interstate. We chose not to complain that our lane had slowed down to 55mph, and we made a mental note to return home by a different route. Our headaches were swelling as our patience was wearing thin. We had more than met our distance goal, and it was time to stop. Senator, who is generally frugal like myself, reasoned that we should look for the most expensive rate, and then get a room at that hotel. (This isn't as decadent as it sounds when rooms start at about $29 per night.) It was not only doable, but it proved to be a great investment as it was one of the quietest nights we have ever spent in a hotel. Gradually our heads recovered.

Sunday we felt better. We were ready to take on the mere five hours of remaining driving time to reach Grandma's house. We were even ready to take on the predicted rain. I wasn't sure we were ready to take on the predicted tornadoes however, so we left early enough to beat the worst weather. Mostly we encountered drizzle, and more people who, for reasons beyond comprehension, decided they should operate vehicles at high speeds, despite lack of skill. Finally, we arrived.

It was satisfying to feel the ocean breeze, even if storms were coming in. It was also satisfying to see Grandma, who never seems to change, one of life's comforting constants. We hugged her and lugged our bags inside, noticing all of her picture-perfect landscaping. I was glad that we had not planned much this trip. I was already tired. Casual visiting and a few park explorations seemed the perfect agenda.

We parked ourselves in the oversized living room recliners and began to chat. Before long the conversation fell off to the rhythm of the rain, which had quickly moved from sprinkle to downpour. The stage was set for a much needed nap, so we yielded. The cat, uninterested up to this point, approved of the idea and found a suitable lounging spot for himself as well.

It was late afternoon when we woke up, and the rain had not missed a beat. Sheets of water were coming down with no end in sight. Ahhh, sunny Florida. *Well that's one day I don't have to wear sunscreen.*

We were all getting hungry, which led to the question of where to grab some dinner. Conveniently, there were the THE COUPONS. Grandma had won some gift cards for a local family restaurant as a result of a hot night at bingo, so we decided to give it a try. Just before leaving, I noticed that the gift cards had expired the day before. We certainly did not care, as we had intended to put up a good fight to buy dinner, but it bothered Grandma.* With a mutter of disgust, she tossed them down on the counter. The cat looked up questioningly, but not upset enough to actually produce movement on his part.

We headed for the intended restaurant, discount notwithstanding. The parking lot at the restaurant was completely flooded. Senator dropped us off at the door and joined us after parking in the shallowest spot. The were no other customers, which made me wonder a bit, but a sweet hostess sat us with a warm welcome. Grandma told her about the gift card dilemma, and she said she would still honor THE COUPONS. O happy day.... except they were on the counter at home. Well, that settled it; we would just have to come back another time within the next three days.

Soon our food arrived, and I was pleasantly surprised. A spicy black bean and egg burrito was brimming with plenty of fresh veggies. We dove into warm cheese and salsa. Set off with

---

*What is it that makes consumers yield to the gravitational pull of coupon usage? Sure we save money, but it is more than that. There is the supreme thrill of conquering. You possess the knowledge that, due to some cosmic fortune, some twist of fate, you will be enjoying the same quality product as the poor saps who are paying full price. You have not cheated, and yet you have come out ahead in the barter. Suddenly you are primally connected to the first caveperson who traded only six shells for two turtles, when everyone clearly agreed that the going rate was eight shells. You have beaten the system. You have won.

a weak cup of diner coffee, and rain constantly washing down the window of the booth, it made for a very cozy meal. We finished and sloshed out through the growing puddles.

Back at the house, I immediately changed into lounging clothes. There is something very comforting about laying around in one's jammies at one's grandma's house. The feeling does not change whether you are two years old or... well, my age. It was my defiant proclamation that I was on vacation, even though I was about to seclude myself with social studies notes. At least I was reviewing constitutional amendments and African trade patterns with palm trees in the background.

As I studied, I could hear muffled television voices in the next room. Senator was relaxing with Grandma as she flipped through the channels. Not having television at home, this is all part of the 'when in Rome' experience for us. For lack of a better option, they settled on *The Apprentice*, a reality show that pitted celebrities against each other as they vied for Donald Trump's affection, or at least another week as his employee.

I soon heard a familiar voice. Interrupted by the recognition, I glanced up from my lengthy geography notes which explained (in detail) the difference between 'location' and 'place'.* On the television, nobly blathering something about wanting to be a strong team and feeling that everyone needed to come together and do his or her part, was former Illinois governor Rod Blagojevich.

If you are unfamiliar with the epic drama, it can be summed up in one sentence: 'Blago' utilized standard Chicago political methods to try to auction off Obama's old senate seat to the highest bidder. No, I don't mean he tried to sell an antique chair; he tried to sell a powerful position, correctly observing that it was, "f---ing golden". Since being indicted by the Feds, his

---

* Oh yes. There *is* a difference., but you have to look it up for yourself.

mission has been to use any possible public forum to proclaim his innocence and remind the Illi-noid of all the wonderful things he has supposedly done for us.

Now he was walking the streets of New York, shaking as many hands as possible on the way to Trump's offices. His standard greeting was, "Hi, I'm Rod Blagojevich, and I didn't do anything wrong!" Nothing like making your moment count. I guess you need all the help you can get when five minutes of the show's time allotment are devoted to the fact that it took you thirty minutes to type a short paragraph. Ever the excuse-monger, he reasoned that, "When you're governor, you have, like 60,000 people under you. You don't have to do these things." Need I say more?

Eventually I finished my good girl studying and joined Grandma and Senator. *What's that you say, Grandma?* It was unanimously declared dessert time, so we plunged into Grandma's angel food cake with strawberries. As I may have explained in previous books, I have a theory about the body:soul food compatibility ratio. Generally, there is food that is good for the body, and food that is bad for the body. If, however, said negative food warms the soul to a level greater than the physical damage it may create, it is determined to be a beneficial food, and should be enjoyed as such. In layman's terms, dessert eaten while sitting in your pajamas at your Grandma's should be consumed without restraint or guilt... even if it's fifteen minutes before you go to bed.

Monday morning the sky had cleared. Sun and a powerful wind did their best to dry things out from the previous day's four inches of rain. Like the staged commercials, we woke up to the smell of freshly brewed coffee. It took me a moment to realize where I was. When I did get my bearings, I popped out of bed to pour two cups of java. Senator soon followed.

The great thing about a day off, especially when one is on vacation, is that there is a distinct difference between getting *up* and getting *going*. We got up, got our coffee, and then met Grandma on the back porch to watch the birds, the water, the chameleons, and anything else that was moving faster than us. It was quite some time before we got going. As a hyperproductive, goal-oriented multitasker who favors her German quarter, it almost frightens me how easily I can settle into lounge mode.

When the spirit moved us to get going, we were ready to walk. We started by driving to The Pier, (whose name never ceases to amaze me for its sheer lack of imagination). Here, I offer a word of advice. If you dislike crowds, but like the occasional tourist attraction, try going on a Monday morning. People are either too busy, tired, broke, or hung over from their weekend to go out. As a record show dealer so eloquently put it once, when a show was extremely empty, "You could throw a grenade in here and only kill, like, three people!"

We walked the quiet levels of The Pier, taking in the 360° view. Some sailboats ventured out, an easy target for the whipping winds. To the southwest we could see race cars speeding around a track. The St. Petersburg Grand Prix had been rained out the day before, and now drivers from all over the country were antsy to burn rubber. We should have entered the Yaris, except we might risk going airborne once we topped 100mph.

We took our time strolling the long avenue that led to the car. On the way back, we stopped off to check the bicycle rental situation. At home, it was still too cold to ride bikes, and we were starting to feel the urge pretty heavily. Looking over our options, though, there were only two kinds: large adult bicycles, or dumb family bike-things. The large bikes were out of the question for my stubby legs, and the dumb family bike-things lived up to their name. Although, I guess if your idea of fun is to cram four or five people under a canopy while trying to simultaneously pedal and steer the awkward beast, go for it. Just watch those corners; they can be a bugger to maneuver. *Whoops!*

There goes little Joey.

Shelving the bike rental idea, Grandma, Senator, and I departed for our next destination. I had remembered going to Weedon Island as a child, guided by Papa, our fearless leader. I knew it as a wild expanse of land along the water, a swampy prairie, if such a thing exists. It was a wonderful, out-of-the-way place reserved just for us. But then, my mind has painted every excursion with Papa as magical.

I braced the door as I got out of the car. Long hair flailed in all directions. Weedon Island had been tamed a bit in recent years. A boardwalk now ran from the visitor center throughout the park. Guide signs informed, educated, and kept one safe from adventure. Still, the ponds were beautiful, and the fish still jumped. Thankfully, no one had coerced the trees to behave. Palms continued to sprawl like fireworks frozen in time, and Spanish moss swayed from ancient branches of native trees. Plus, there was the added excitement of a snake[*] slithering just off the trail, and wading through overgrown puddles in flooded areas. Overall, I was satisfied.

After leaving Weedon Island, we made a pit stop for a few groceries. Assembling odds and ends, we had plenty for a picnic lunch in the screen room back at Grandma's house. For weeks before arriving, she had asked me what food to have on hand, and I had always dodged the question, not wanting anyone to go through any trouble to accommodate our specific dietary habits. I think she was convinced we would starve. Now she could see that, yes, we were well fed, even if our sprouts, cole slaw, chips, giardiniera, and fruit did not always resemble a traditional meal. *Crazy kids.*

There was one more park that Senator and I wanted to visit. Sawgrass County Park is known for its lush vegetation and

---

[*] Sizewise, Senator would describe it as "considerable", Grandma would say "pretty big", and I would say "enormous".

wildlife, including alligators. This seems especially surreal since you drive through a regular suburban neighborhood to get there. At what would seem to be a dead end lies the entrance.

Five minutes into our walk we saw a dining cormorant. If you have never seen a Japanese cormorant swallow a fish, you would not think it possible. First of all, they do not choose small, elongated fish. This particular bird had a round, flat fish about the size of a small dinner plate. They also do not bother to break up their food. Just like a cartoon, the bird's skinny neck swells as the oversized meal can be seen wriggling its way down to the stomach. How a cormorant can breathe during this process I do not know. Grandma told us that Japanese fishermen used to tie string around the birds' necks so they could extract whole fish after the cormorants had done the hard part. Just another hassle vegetarians manage to avoid.

As I mentioned, Sawgrass is known primarily for its alligator population. We had spotted one or two when we visited in 2006. I have also seen other alligators while visiting Florida as a kid.* While it is always a little eerie when you first notice the motionless creatures sunning themselves, common sense and logical distance keep the observer safe.

It made me very nervous, however, to watch the six- or seven- year old boy whose dad took him entirely too close for comfort. Hungry alligators have been known to snatch both animals and people if the opportunity arises, and it would have been a simple feat in this case. I was weak in the knees until the boy finally left. *Some parents just suck.*

Our park-hopping adventure was over, and it was time for more mindless reality television, and perhaps a bite to eat. Apparently the new season of *Dancing With the Stars* was afoot,

---

* Though its jaws were tightly duct taped shut, my mother winced to watch my four-year old brother and my eight-year old self hold a baby alligator while on a family vacation once.

and the entire senior citizen demographic of Florida was rooting for astronaut Buzz Aldrin as he performed his best moves on the dance floor. He was no Fred Astaire, but did I mention that he walked on the moon?! What could be more graceful? Although, he did famously remark that walking on the moon was "a piece of cake" compared to dancing on the show. So our first full day in Florida concluded with the three of us indulging in pizza while watching an eighty-year old national hero attempt to tango. God bless America!

As I have mentioned, this trip was low-key, and for the most part, unscheduled. Beside the parks that we had tackled, I simply wanted to visit my great-uncle, who also lives in St. Petersburg. Uncle Bud[*] was eighty-five years old, going on sixty-five. Thanks to a daily regimen of a long walk and a glass of orange juice produced by his own trees, more than a few of the senior ladies have their eyes on Uncle Bud. Like all of the members of my grandma's family, he is always smiling, giving, sharing a joke, or telling a great story.

After a walk and a juice of our own, Grandma, Senator, and I hopped in the car for the short ride down 4th Street. After many stop-and-gos at traffic lights, we came to Uncle Bud's street. The white house that once belonged to my great-grandparents in their retirement years still sat in its familiar, pretty place, complete with palms in the front. Descendents of the chameleons that my great grandma loved scurried around the patio blocks.[†] Uncle Bud, the relaxed Floridian, yelled for us to come in, teasing his little sister a bit upon entry.

My eyes wandered the living room, remembering a faint

---

[*] Which-- don't ask me how-- is derived from his given name, George

[†] Grandma tells the story of her mother rolling tiny balls of raw hamburger and leaving them out for the chameleons to eat. One day, when Great-Grandpa was sitting out in the sunny yard with his shirt off, a chameleon ran up his chest and bit him, mistaking a nipple for one of the usual treats.

scene with my great-grandparents and their immense (or so it seemed) grandfather clock. I also saw the arched doorway that seemed so unique and archaic to a girl who grew up in a modern house. In the midst of this, my great-grandparents did not seem too far away.* Now Senator was with me and we found our places around the informal kitchen table. I think we may have all been barefoot.

Before we got too far into conversation, Uncle Bud ushered us up again to see the latest renovation. A talented handyman, he had added a second bathroom which almost doubled the master bedroom. The roomy shower and soft décor could have been featured in an elegant home magazine. *Could I ever be this productive in my 80s?* After much admiration, we returned to our kitchen perches.

Somehow we wove between three generations of memories of the Joliet area from which we all hailed. As is always the case with 'the world's biggest small town', familiar surnames were swapped and there were many good stories to accompany them. Even as an avid rodent lover, I did not envy my uncle's tale of taking large boards to work to protect himself from overgrown wild rats. *No thanks. The pet shop variety was good enough for me.* This also prompted him to remind us that there was a special documentary on rats on television later that night.

Uncle Bud then asked what we had done in town so far. When we mentioned going to parks, it provided him with a segue into his next story. Recently his family had been in town, and they had wanted to visit Fort De Soto, a historic and lovely setting for wading and picnics. While they were all in the car, he

---

* While I do not believe in ghosts in the traditional Hollywood sense, I do believe that some people live so vibrantly that they leave indelible impressions on the places they frequented. Scientific, no. Romantic, perhaps. Apparent to me, absolutely.

started to give them directions. They quickly shut him down, explaining that they had a GPS system that would guide them step-by-step. As they drove miles in the opposite direction of the park, Uncle Bud just smiled and kept his mouth shut. After the frustration of not finding anything that resembled a beach or a fort, the kids admitted defeat. Man won out over machine when they realized that the GPS had neatly guided them to the park *offices*, which were located at the exact opposite end of town.

After chatting some more, Uncle Bud offered us fresh grapefruit from his backyard trees. Heck yeah! We filled as many bags as we could carry, as he profusely apologized that there were not more. This would be our consolation prize if the weather was still crummy when we got back home. Reader, if you have never eaten citrus fresh off the tree, start making friends with a few kind Floridians. You may never drink grocery store juice again!

There was time for just one more story before leaving. Uncle Bud remarked about the little animals that were occasionally seen around the street. "We don't often get rabbits, but we had one around for a while," he started. "The neighbors mentioned it to each other if they saw it, and it became sort of a collective mascot. It would sometimes dart in the street, but everyone was careful, until one day, when someone hit it and killed it." You might think this would be the sad part of the story, until Uncle Bud, through giggles, clarified that it was a young humane society worker that ran it over. "The poor girl was so upset! We tried to calm her down and help her pull herself together, but she took it pretty hard." Naturally, we laughed hysterically at this. Sometimes even cruel irony is just plain funny!

We fumbled our grapefruit as we hugged Uncle Bud good-bye. No one needs to convince me that he and Grandma are part of the Greatest Generation. So many people their age have worked their way through drastic hardships, maintaining their sense of humor and core values all the way through. They are a standard by which we can gain a more meaningful perspective. I sometimes shutter to think what my generation's legacy will be...

Of course, not *every* senior is so enlightened. As we turned into the gated entry of Grandma's neighborhood (cruising speed: 8mph), a man on a bike yelled at me for not using my blinker in a lane that only curved to the left. "Try blinkers-- they work!" he snapped. *Hhmmm, good use of sarcasm, Sir. Alright, Pal.* There's a sin I will never commit again.

Back at the house, I ruefully remembered my study notes. I was not sure I cared about socioeconomic electoral patterns that afternoon. Again, I tempered the task by studying in a room full of windows. Perhaps all a person really needs is a room with a view.

The breeze and sun felt good on the not-too-hot day. Senator and Grandma ventured outside to read. I think this may have involved closed eyes and a soft snore or two. They needed their rest, though. After all, we had a busy night ahead of us.

When I had sufficiently talked myself into believing I had studied enough, I joined my two lounging buddies. I suppose we threw something together for dinner, but it was inconsequential. The highlight of the evening was the simultaneous viewing of *Dancing With the Stars* and the rat documentary Uncle Bud had suggested. In an age of on-demand television and recorded programming, the art of channel flipping is sometimes lost in favor of relaxed, chronological viewing. Not so here. We would watch a few moments of a lovely gowned diva waltzing across a stage, only to be replaced by a litter of newborn ratlettes a brief remote control click later.

We saw overworked and undertalented dancers in tears because they received low scores from judges. Then we saw overworked and underfed Asian villagers in tears because they would likely lose the year's crop to the rapidly expanding rodent population. It was an odd pairing to be sure, but it was also a great illustration of how trivial the concerns of a wealthy nation can be. Frankly, I preferred the rats to most of the dancers.

Just when we were getting the rhythm of channel surfing down, we decided we needed to expand the entertainment. It had been four years since we rolled the dice to a good game of Yahtzee with Grandma. As we played a 'refresher round', we glanced from score card to dice cup to television.[*] I don't remember who won, but I do remember the cat being intrigued at the white cubes with the crazy black dots that we kept throwing around. *Why don't I have any toys like that?* he seemed to be thinking.

When the dancers had taken their bows and the fields had been saved from the hungry swarms of rats and the Yahtzee scores had been tallied, we settled into the easy chairs. The nightly news droned on in the background. Somewhere a disgruntled employee had shot her young boss. Elsewhere the weather was iffy. In our cozy setting, however, I refused to believe any of it was real. All I knew was that our time at Simple Pleasures Central was slipping away fast. We were at the halfway point of our vacation. Finally, I was starting to relax.

Wednesday morning started off with what else, but orange juice from Uncle Bud's trees. Senator is an extremely easy travel companion, and he faithfully goes along with any plans I make, but this was his day. While reading an article in a music magazine a few months earlier, he had stumbled upon the surprising fact that the world's largest record store[†] existed in St.

---

[*] I should mention that my grandma is one of the great multitaskers of our time. It is not unusual for her to be simultaneously watching television, reading the newspaper, listening to a ballgame on the radio, and talking on the phone, never missing a beat in the conversation. If she were a CEO, the company's work week would surely be down to three days.

[†] fact not verified

Petersburg, Florida, of all places. Taking it as a divine sign to go on a vinyl quest, we packed a street map and some cash. An hour later we were in a musty warehouse of wonders.

We located the obscure Bananas compound at the end of what looked like a small industrial park. A steep outdoor staircase led to the first of two buildings. Across the street sat the other. This could take a while.

We climbed the stairs and entered the maze of a room. Tight rows of shelves were packed from floor to well over my head. The owners had managed to collect both rare pieces and great quantities of common vinyl titles. The twentysomething guy at the desk grunted a "Hey" and asked if we were looking for anything in particular. Nope, just browsing. Senator scanned specific areas for good deals or possible resaleables. I lamely flipped through a few rows. I could not even tell you what I saw; there was just too much. Senator's search was not producing the desired results, so we trotted back down the stairs to visit building #2.

Across the street was the Bananas warehouse, complete with open garage doors at each end and a giant fan doing its best to move the rapidly warming air. Within moments, Senator had located the cheap treasures. Now this was more like it. His fingers nimbly ran through the bins, occasionally accompanied by a grin that I knew meant he had spotted a deal. A few times he fired up the cell phone to check in with Chicago pal Anthony[*] about a particular album. Usually this reference resulted in adding another record to the growing stack.

I actually managed to find two books I wanted. Leave it to me to find the one shelf of books among the tens of thousands

---

[*] Anthony's great gift in life is being able to turn bizarre vintage media into profits... which he then spends on bizarre vintage media. My favorite Anthony success story: Catholic coloring books. If you have to ask, you're obviously going to Purgatory.

of records. Once I had exhausted that brief project, however, I started to fade out. I weasled the keys out of Senator's pocket and kissed him good-bye and good luck. "I'm going out to the car to take a nap."

Don't get me wrong; I'm not naïve. I knew that my being out of sight would render me out of mind, thereby stopping the passage of time in Senator's consciousness. Without me wandering aimlessly within view, he would easily become engrossed in the hunt. And I was glad. He deserved to get lost in the enjoyment of music and memories. I kicked off my shoes and reclined the seat.

I was just about to drift off to a breezy car nap when I caught a strange glimpse in the rear view mirror. I sat up and turned around to see if I had started dreaming prematurely. There, cruising down the quiet street, was a man in a motorized, fully reclined easy chair. His feet were up and his head was shaded by a small umbrella-- the very picture of contentment. He carelessly clipped by at about 10mph.

I could only imagine what must have gone through his mind as he created his stylish transportation. *Let's see-- I need to get around, but not everything is within walking distance. Cars are too expensive, and it's not like it's going to get cold. I suppose I could get a bike, but they're so, well, common.* As he sat in his living room, suddenly it struck him. Why not move this perfectly suitable and versatile furniture outdoors... and add wheels and a motor? Eureka! The Reclinocycle is born!

I slunk back down in the front seat and dozed for a while. Eventually Senator came out, smiling and armed with a hefty stack of records. He couldn't wait to sort through his new acquisitions. I just wish he had seen the Reclinocycle.

When we arrived at Grandma's, she had lunch ready to go in the screen room. I lingered there as long as possible before going to gather my study notes. This time I was not messing around. I plopped myself down outside, only feet from the water, in full view of the diving osprey and jumping fish. Senator, who declared that he, too, needed to 'study', wasted no time in taking off his glasses and laying his head in my lap. My handful of notes conveniently blocked the sun from his eyes. A short moment later, his breathing was as slow and rhythmic as the lightly splashing waves. I wondered whether such tranquil conditions would help my brain absorb the information. Time would tell.

When Grandma stepped out onto the back porch, she laughed at our arrangement. The unused chairs surrounded us as we sprawled out on the floor. "How is the studying coming, Honey?"

"Great-- I saw an osprey catch a fish, and I waved to your neighbors as they came back from boating." So much for intense academics. Senator woke up and we all found a spot to read magazines. I looked from my bare legs to Grandma's. No question as to which one of us spends her winters in the Midwest. My well-preserved paleness gleamed in the bright sun.

Before we knew it, a few hours had passed. We broke ranks to get ready to go out to dinner. This was the chosen night for Operation Gift Card. You will recall, Reader, that on our first night in Florida Grandma was determined to use some gift card coupons that she had won. Though recently expired, the manager gave her the thumbs up to bring them in. We returned to the family restaurant and were seated in a booth.

Here our server apprised us of the fact that it was Free Slice of Pie Night. We would each get our choice of pie with our dinner. Bonus! After ordering and consuming another tasty meal, the dessert and coffee came. I was probably the only person in the place that jumped at the chance to eat pumpkin pie in March. Out of season plus free equals even more delicious than when eaten at Thanksgiving.

When we had eaten the last forkfuls* of pie, Grandma asked our server for the bill. I noticed that it was about $32. I don't give numbers to be impolite, but to illustrate the crazy math that then ensued. As we went to the front to pay, Grandma decided to purchase a pie to go, to have on hand for her next round of company. This took the bill to about $42. She then produced $10 worth of gift card coupons. Reasonably this should have led to a $32 balance, but somewhere in the space-time continuum the accounting went awry. The cashier could not figure out how to ring the extra pie and the gift cards. Neither could the other cashier. By the time the manager got involved, the register transaction had been so confused and abused that they handed Grandma her pie, telling her it was on the house because of the confusion. It was a generous and unexpected gesture, that should have brought the bill down to $22. After more button punching and spewing of receipts however, the manager pronounced the balance to be $15. "Are you sure? I think it should be more," Grandma offered.

"Nope. It says here $15," he responded. Good enough for us. She paid the man and we left the restaurant, halfway feeling like thieves, considering all the free pie and discounts. The food is great and the staff is very friendly, but I doubt they will be in business much longer with that kind of math.

The evening progressed with a few rounds of Yahtzee and some unmemorable television. We were sure living up the night life in St. Petersburg. In fact, we did so much nothing that I wondered if this chapter would be more than a couple of pages long. Near the end of the night though, a shocking announcement was made.

"I think I'm going to go to that Dali museum with you tomorrow," Grandma declared quite out of the blue. We had

---

* spoonful in my case. Forks are only for food that you don't mind losing between the tines.

extended the invitation several times to go to the Salvador Dali Museum with us, but each time she wrinkled her nose and explained that she thought he was kind of weird. "No, I don't really care for his stuff. You kids go and have fun," was her standard reply.

"That's wonderful! What made you change your mind?" I asked.

"Well, I was just thinking that I'm almost eighty-four years old, and I've never been there, and I should try new things. If I hate it, at least I can say I gave it a try." I couldn't have said it better myself. If only my high school students had this type of ambitious attitude. See what I mean about this Greatest Generation?

"I'm so excited that you've decided to come! If nothing else, at least you can always make fun of his mustache," I reasoned, throwing my index fingers upward from the sides of my mouth in homage to the famous Dali photograph.*

With that, we said our goodnights and went to bed. It was not a restful night for me, though. Several times throughout the night, I twisted and turned to work out a painful kink in the right side of my back. Senator, sensing my movement, reached out blindly to assist by rubbing my back. He did not have to ask where; a few swipes of his large hands covers the entirety of my back. I whispered, "Thank you," but the effect was temporary. By morning I was hurting.

Hoping to stretch out whatever was crunched up, I suggested a walk. Grandma and Senator joined me in winding in and out of the lanes of Americana Cove. On my feet, I felt fine. I wasn't so sure what would happen when I sat down, though. In the last few minutes of our walk, we passed Dave and Jane's house. Grandma yelled, "Hello" when she recognized

---

* At press time, Salvador Dali's Mustache even has its own Facebook page.

a silhouette reading in the screen room.

"Oh, haw-ya doin' Dara-thee!" came the heavily Massachusan reply.

"C'mon out and meet the kids," called Grandma. *I love being 'the kids'.*

"Nope, no kids!" joked Dave as he opened the door to greet us.

They invited us in, but Grandma explained that we were just stopping for a moment. "Besides, guess where we have to go today?"

"Ah have no idear. Where ya gawin' Dara-thee?"

"Going to see Dali!" Grandma beamed proudly, the newest member of the Surrealist Appreciation Society of Seniors.[*]

Dave wrinkled up his nose. "Dahw-li? What do ya wanna see him fah?" Grandma relayed her because-I'm-almost-eighty-four reasoning. Unconverted, Dave replied, "No, nevah cahed fah him. Have fun, though. You'll have to tell us awl about him."

We chatted for a few more minutes and then said goodbye. I have met Dave and Jane a few times, and I always enjoy them. They are pleasant, funny, and well, New Englanders. "Hey Dara-thee, see if ya can fix his mustache!" Dave laughed at having the last word as we walked down the block.

While Dali was the main event, we found ourselves with plenty of time to kill until we had to leave for the museum. Grandma went in the house to do Grandma things while Senator and I grabbed reading material and headed for the porch by the water. Yes, I said reading. I grandly declared that I was taking the day off from studying. Senator heartily approved.

A few minutes into our reading a strange man walked into the yard. Then another. I was a little startled at first because the area is private and certainly not on the way to anywhere else.

---

[*] SASS for short.

Neither man spoke English well, but soon their interpreter came around. Of course-- it was Sod Patch Day.

Florida had endured a rough (for them) winter, which left several dead patches of grass. In other words, they had occasional spots in their yards that looked worse than the rest of the grass, but still far better than anything Illinois had seen in six months. Apparently getting the replacement was a big deal. The next door neighbors were delighted, especially when the landscapers put in more good sod than they were supposed to.

While the ecstasy of new grass somewhat escaped us,* we had our own thrill. Senator pointed out an distinct triangle cutting through the water. It sure looked like a dark gray fin to me. Soon it rose up in a graceful arch just above the surface. A dolphin was swimming in the inlet, approaching the dock swiftly. Senator stood at the edge for a better look. I then noticed a few more dolphins in the distance. This one however, set its eyes on Senator and swam up to make a fast friend. I had never seen a wild dolphin so close. Maybe he/she was welcoming us, or asking to play, or plotting to takeover the humans as soon as opposable thumbs could be obtained. At any rate, we were mutually fascinated by one another.

As the dolphins were swimming out to the open water, a pontoon boat was coming in. I waved out of habit. The boaters waved back and smiled. Then we heard a familiar holler. "Hawse Daw-li? Did ya see him yet?" Dave teased as he maneuvered his boat toward their dock. Grandma just shook her head and laughed. Actually, it was just about time to go surrealizing, so we left for the museum.

Here, I am embarrassed to admit that I let traffic stress get

---

* This love of grass was ironic as my whole mission each growing season is to rip out more grass and replace it with plants. Of course, that could be because I have more weeds in a square foot of my grass than Grandma has on her entire property.

to me. In downtown St. Petersburg the one-way streets were not intuitive, and not conducive to the planned route. Pedestrians who stepped obliviously out into the street did not help, either. *One of these clowns is going to end up looking like a flat, melting clock if they don't watch where they're going.*

Once we arrived, I was fine. The museum bordered a marina, and the horizon was filled with sailboats. The ocean breeze followed us up to the ticket counter. "One senior, one adult, and one teacher, please," I requested, producing my ugly school i.d. card to save two bucks. We took our tickets and entered the first gallery.

We had fifteen minutes to kill until our tour began, so we checked out the local student art on the walls. The depth and detail was impressive. I thought that perhaps art school pieces were featured, but these surrealist adaptations were produced by the area's high schoolers. I had never seen such advanced work from teenagers. Maybe the warm weather keeps the hands nimble and the fingers agile.

Suddenly a short, tanned, middle-aged man with a thick New York accent spoke up to gather the group's attention. We formed a loose semicircle around him as he explained the origins of the museum. Years ago a wealthy Ohio couple had taken a liking to Dali's keys and skinny-legged giraffes and crucifixes and decided to become his patrons. Thus, we may behold magnificent works of art that may otherwise have been lost.

Our tour guide's animated character continued. "Now there are many hidden meanings in Daw-li's work. Some I will explain; othuhs I will leave tah ya imagination. There is awlso a lot of erotica and sexuality, but we won't go intah that since theh ah kids on the tou-ah." Adults looked around, trying to determine which tour members were depriving us of the gems of information that our guide had to offer. The few kids in the company looked crestfallen at 1.)being singled out as immature art critics, and 2.)missing out on some good sex stories, inexplicably having something to do with a girl named Erica.

The tour progressed through several galleries, each displaying intricate works of vibrant color and multiple layers of objects and meaning. A smaller painting interwove the three stages of life: infancy, adolescence, and old age. I'm afraid to ask where I fit into that. A mural-sized work, upon further inspection, revealed three crucifixes in a tribute to Columbus. Finally, in one of my personal favorites, the aptly name *Hallucinogenic Toreador*, bullfighters melt easily into copies of the Venus de Milo. And this is all I'm allowed to tell you. Perhaps I've already said too much...

We spent a little more time viewing the paintings on our own. Grandma had become hooked. She was trying to remember when the guide had said Dali was born. "Was it 1900?" I asked. We walked over to ask the guide.

"Salvador Daw-li was born on May 11, 1904." We both let out a yelp. The guide looked surprised, wondering what could be so special about the date.

"I was born on May 11th!" Grandma explained. "Although, much later, of course," she quickly added. In twenty-four hours she had gone from Dali detractor to a birthday buddy.

Riding high on the new found fact, we walked to the back room theatre for a showing of the A&E Biography of Salvador Dali, complete with popcorn. The room filled quickly with fans seated in all of the chairs, and on the floor. As expected, Dali's life was atypical. He started out with a comfortable upbringing, but clearly did not view the world as his peers did. Soon he met Gala, the self-appointed manager/lover/mother figure who formed the framework of most of the rest of his life. She demanded of him an excellence that propelled him almost beyond himself, if such a thing is possible. His home eventually took on a circus atmosphere of bizarre parties with unexpected guests.

Friends as varied as veteran rock frontman Alice Cooper became close to Dali. In fact, Dali honored the friendship by creating a hologram depicting Cooper's brain-- a strange, rotating image of Cooper, seated, with his brain poised behind his head.* Upon presentation of a model of the piece, Cooper commented on its artistic merit and asked if he could have it. Dali, practical in all matters of his works' value, snapped back, "Of course not! It's worth millions!"

No, Dali was not the standard starving artist. He had no problem whipping out tens of thousands of prints for the sake of easy money. He also bypassed the expensive drug habit to which so many artists fall prey. When asked if the popular psychadelic drugs of the day had a hand in his work, he scoffed, "I *am* L.S.D.!" Apparently he was doing something right, at least in the financial management realm; at his death, Salvador Dali had $100,000,000 in the bank.

With our art appreciation crash course behind us, we left the museum in search of a bite to eat. Nothing sounded particularly tempting until Grandma remembered hearing good things about Paisano's. I liked the sound of it. We have yet to go wrong with Italian, so we pulled into the shared parking lot.

The little Italian restaurant was unassumingly tucked into a strip mall. Once inside, though, the atmosphere was casual but classy. Scenes of grapes and wine bottles lined the room. More importantly, scenes of cheese and tomatoes lined the menu. I highly recommend the fresh and delicious calzones. With stuffed bellies and the realization that our stay was almost over, we went back to Grandma's house for one last night of mindless relaxation.

Again the pajamas and television went on. This time there were no celebrities or struggling farmers. On the screen

---

*Actually entitled *First Cylindric Chromo-Hologram Portrait of Alice Cooper's Brain*

were beautiful scenes from America's national parks. I can get lost in these kinds of shows, imagining myself at Yellowstone or in the Great Smoky Mountains. On that night, however, I was in even deeper. My breathing slowed down as I snuggled sideways in the overstuffed chair. I trailed off quickly to a soft-spoken narrator's recital of a Teddy Roosevelt quote.

Friday morning had come fast, as expected. Thanks to a light schedule, however, we were well rested and ready to head homeward. Still, I am never ready to say good-bye to Grandma. For as long as I can remember, being with her has symbolized joy and an innocent fun that seems harder and harder to come by in a cynical world.

Senator fit the suitcase in the trunk between boxes of records and bags of grapefruit. He then swung around to open my door, as is his custom. I hugged Grandma once more, glad that she would be back in Illinois soon. She wished me luck on my upcoming test. *Oh yeah... that.* I wasn't even sure I cared much anymore. At the moment, I was just glad that my back was feeling better, and that we had enjoyed such a relaxing visit. As we backed out of the short driveway, I waved contentedly.

Once on the highway, I checked the leash again. I had been checking our home answering machine daily via the cell phone, just in case there were any messages regarding potential teaching jobs. Nothing. Same as the rest of the week. Oh, well-- on to April.

Against our better judgment, we drove into Georgia, instead of taking a different route home. Traffic was cruising along quickly until we were about forty miles south of Atlanta. There things slowed. Soon we were at a crawl. Why in the world had I fallen for optimism? It was so unlike me. For a deluded few hours I truly believed that this would be the better route because, even if traffic slowed somewhat, it was still considerably shorter than going through Alabama.

The solid mass of automobiles scraped along, congesting

on and off ramps alike. The longer we sat, the closer to rush hour it became. Adding more commuters into the mix was not making anyone's day brighter. Finally we exited to a bypass. Contrary to the name, the only thing we passed by was more time, sitting frustrated in the traffic jam. So *this* time when we promised ourselves to never take I-75 through Georgia during spring break season, we meant it!

When we finally got out of Georgia, the sun was slipping away quickly, and the horizon held plenty of Tennessee drivers. In and out of the hill passes they darted. We kept pace, carefully guarding against the occasional truck that would claim a larger territory than its lane permitted. My vision of making it to Nashville was fading fast. Around 7:30pm, Senator declared that hillbillies on curving roads, after dark, often with a good Friday night buzz, were not inspiring his great confidence for our safety. Driving was done for the day. We would take the next exit that had lodging... provided we could not hear any banjos.

The lonely, dark exit in eastern Tennessee led us to what would be a main street through town, if, in fact, there were a town of which to speak. One side of the highway was empty, trailing off into the hills. The other side hosted the Smokehouse Lodge compound, complete with inn, restaurant, and country store. We pulled into the neatly kept and well lit parking lot.

The lodge half of the Smokehouse Lodge was made of large timbers, with homey local accents. Everything seemed clean, which is always a good sign. We also noticed that the place was pretty full. At least there would be plenty of witnesses if we somehow disappeared among the hills, ne'er to return Yankeeward again.

After a few minutes of language barrier deconstruction, the friendly desk clerk sold us a room. We took our key and walked outside to the log staircase that led to the balcony. Our second floor room was around back. The night air was getting thick, as rain was on its way in. The air was also heavy with the smokehouse half of the Smokehouse Lodge. Judging from the smell, I suspected they would smoke anything that could be killed without putting up too much of a fight.

Our room was simple, clean, and comfortable. Now on to item number two: food. We had nibbled a little in the car, but we had not really eaten all day. Since we left home, almost a week earlier, I had been craving Mexican food. Lately I had been making it a lot at home, and I needed my fix of beans, cheese, and salsa. While eastern Tennessee is not particularly known for its south-of-the-border cuisine, we gave the phone book a try.

"Actually, it shows a place about two miles down the road," offered Senator. It should still be open for another hour." That was good enough for me. After a brief pit stop, we left the room and exited to the Balcony of Smoked Carcass.

In a few minutes we were in the car. I wondered if the road would magically reveal more signs of life just two miles away. There sure weren't any lights welcoming us as we left the inn behind. *Maybe we should have stuck with the cashews and raisins that were still tucked in my purse.*

Just then we saw the promised Mexican restaurant on the left side of the road. The parking lot was hopping, and I noticed license plates from several different states in the southeast. Several men talked and laughed as they smoked in a screened-in lounge facing the parking lot. So this was where they kept all the tourists who decided not to brave the hillbilly drivers.

As we approached the door it was very loud, but it was not all voices. Instead of mariachi music, a speaker in the entryway was blaring *Your Cheatin' Heart*. Opening the dining room door revealed an all-white staff of southern honies. Nope. Wrong vibes here. If we're going to eat Mexican food cooked by gringos, we will make it ourselves... sans Hank Williams, muchas gracias. We returned to the car and decided to take a brave plunge. Onward to the Smokehouse!

Upon entering the Smokehouse Lodge restaurant, we

walked through a country store that looked like it never left 1948, save for a few modern novelties. Quilts, old photographs, records, homemade jellies, candies, and a butcher counter stood like relics from a bygone era. At the end of the path was the restaurant. The hostess greeted us with a big smile and an even bigger accent. "Hah! Ya'll want smokin' or nonsmokin'?" For a moment we forgot that this option still exists in many states.

She led us to a small nonsmoking table surrounded by old toys, advertisements, farm gadgets, and photographs on the wall. I noticed that Jack Daniels Hot Sauce held a place of honor on each table, saluting its Tennessee roots. As we waited for our server, we skimmed the menu. As expected, it did not take long. Sometimes being a vegetarian simplifies things.

Soon a cute girl who can truly be described as 'pleasantly plump' popped over to our table. She looked like a teenage Shirley Temple, with an adorable personality to match. *Where exactly did the highway exit sign say we were?* We ordered our waters (hold the Jack), and surveyed the scene further. Booklets at each of the tables highlighted major points of various years. We were reading about the top songs in 1956 (primarily Elvis) when Shirley returned.

Senator and I mutually nodded our heads toward each for the other one to order first. Usually I use this to my advantage, because I always take way too long to decide in a restaurant. This time, though, it was easy. "I'll have a baked potato please, but no bacon bits."

"And I'll just have a cheese omelet," Senator added, "no meat." Our girl scrawled a few things on her green order pad and then slipped over to the next table, which now contained five loud, large ladies out for a good time. (Their order was substantially more smokehouse-worthy.)

We were chatting, eavesdropping on the table o' ladies, and reviewing more of 1956 when our server came back. "Ah just haf ta ay-ask: are ya'll vegetarians?" she ventured.

"Yes, we are," we answered simply.

She beamed with pride at her astute observation skills. "Ah just knew it!" She then bounded off for the kitchen, where, no doubt, news of the freaks at table #10 would spread quickly. I glanced around to see two other girls waiting expectantly behind the cash register. I halfway expected them to come out with a camera and take our picture. Then we would be on the wall with other rare visitors who took a moment to sign a memento before passing back into civilization.

Shortly after, our meals arrived. Shirley presented them graciously, and we thanked her in the same manner. I pictured her lovingly picking off each bacon bit from her strange customer's meal. Say what you will about our humble fare, Reader, but these people really know how to smoke an omelet and a baked potato into a gourmet meal. We tipped generously, positive ambassadors to the six vegetarians who live in Tennessee.

With tummies full, we fell into bed easily. In keeping with our tradition, we checked in with the Weather Channel, but all I could muster when the local forecast jazz came on was a small horizontal shimmy. I was too tired to stand. Outside rain plip-plopped on the window. The Weather Channel informed us that this would soon turn into nasty storms. *Good thing we stopped in Wherever-the-Hell-We-Are.*

At 5:00am we both woke up, ready to go. This is not generally the case as we are not morning people; we were just motivated to get home. I love traveling, and I'm always a little sad when a vacation is over, but once I leave the destination spot, I want to be home as soon as possible. Senator was feeling the same way.

Through the night, we had heard a lot of wind and pouring rain as a storm went through. My thoughts turned to hail, but then I remembered we were driving a rental car, and I mentally crossed that off my list of things to worry about.

Automatically we moved through our abbreviated routine, anxious to get on the road. By 5:30am we were in the car, pulling out onto the dark but quiet interstate.

We were about two hours away from Nashville. By my calculation, we could be home by early evening, if the road cooperated. Senator switched on the radio for a weather report. As large drops began to hit the windshield, the forecast confirmed that Tennessee was in for a washout.

By the time we got to Nashville it was raining hard. Though the sun was up, it had grown darker instead of brighter. The pace of traffic dropped down ten miles per hour slower. Just as interstates converged, and more commuter traffic entered and exited on the ramps, the clouds really unzipped. Everyone's speed dropped again because the lane lines were now submerged, obscuring any lines.

Water fell like sheets. My small, white-knuckled hands held the wheel in a death grip as I sat straight up, eyes wide open, adrenaline pumping. I wished Senator was driving, but there was no way to pull over now. He guided me as best he could, and I prayed for safety and guidance while trying to determine the safest following distance behind a semi. If we were too far behind, I would have absolutely no frame of reference for where the road was, and we could end up in a ditch, or worse. If we were too close, the semi might brake suddenly, and we would be his unintentional cargo. This seemed to go on forever, but I suppose it was only about fifteen or twenty minutes.

Then, just as quickly as the onslaught had begun, it tapered down to a mere downpour. I was so relieved that the windshield wipers-- albeit on their highest setting-- could now keep up. I could actually see the road again. Hello you beautiful lanes!

A few more minutes took the rain down to a drizzle. In the rear view mirror an undefined gray blob was all that was visible of Nashville. It was as though we had driven through a curtain of liquid that surrounded the city. Just six weeks later Nashville would be pummeled again with the worst flooding in its recorded history. Some areas would report a two-day precipitation total of 19 inches of rain. Even the Grand Ole Opry was under ten feet of water. So what we have learned here is that, not only are Senator and I capable of destroying places we *plan* to visit, but we may also leave our devastating mark afterward. *Sigh*

The rest of the ride home was smooth, thankfully. The sun beamed as though there were no clouds on this half of the earth. When we stopped for a sandwich, I gladly gave up the reins to Senator. The pavement was dry, and there was barely any traffic in Kentucky and southern Illinois. He clearly had no qualms about 'making good time', and I was not complaining as we sped along.

Despite the morning's rough start, we were home earlier than expected. As we pulled the car behind our alley garage, I could see that the lilacs had burst open. Glancing at the flower gardens, I noticed the little green nubs that were shooting up through the dirt all around. When the neighbor came by to gab and gossip as we finished unloading, I knew that spring had officially come to our small town. I gave Senator a 'welcome back' smooch. It was good to be home.

Chapter 4
Door #2:
Early July 2010

Florida was relaxing, but as soon as we got home, we once again found ourselves in a whirlwind of activity. Easter, a holiday that seemed like it should still be two months away, was the very next day. A few short weeks later we were on a four day mini-tour of Chicago, Milwaukee, and Madison to record various free jazz artists. A few weeks after that saw the end of the school year, and yet another blink concluded summer school, which only ran during the month of June. In between we had hosted house guests twice, biked many miles, participated in an annual rally to support veterans, and recorded two more concerts.

While nothing was set in stone, it was now rumored that I *would* be rehired for one more school year. One day after biking, I came home to an overly perky message on my answering machine. "Hi Wendy! I'm just calling to congratulate you on your rehiring this year!" *Did he say "rehiring" or "retiring"?* Answering machines are not known for their high fidelity. I had better call him to find out whether to plan for AAP* or AARP†. Fortunately, the former was to be my fate. The only problem was that I was entirely too burned out on the job to think much about it.

Thanks to friends Bill and Marge, I could completely put it out of my mind for a few days. For the third year in a row, they had invited Senator and me to join them for a few days in Door County, Wisconsin. We were particularly eager to go since the previous year's excursion had been canceled. We started to think about how much biking, visiting, game playing, and old movie watching we could squeeze into seventy-two hours.

As I packed our clothes and toys, it occurred to me that everything was going uncharacteristically smoothly for the period before a Senator and Wendy V trip. There were still fifteen hours until departure, but everything in the house was cooperating, and the previous days and weeks had been very enjoyable. Two days earlier we had seen an eagle while biking, and later we had fun watching a friend's punk band play. Then I had a blast at a music festival with my dad and my brother. Come to think of it, it was a darn near-perfect week. Throughout all of this, amazingly, there were no reports of crises in Wisconsin or disasters at home. Usually by this point there would be some pre-trip catastrophe, large or small. Good; it was about time.

Eventually Senator came home. It was great to see him after we had spent our annual night apart for Cornerstone Festival. He hugged me and something jabbed me. *Hello?* He grandly presented the Barnes & Noble technological darling, the Nook. The Nook is an electronic reader that allows you to hold a slim metal fake book in your hand and read words on a screen,

---

* Attendance Advocacy Program (the name of the alternative education program I teach to high school seniors)

† American Association of Retired Persons

60

thereby saving you the physical effort and romance of reading a paper book. "I'm bringing one million books along on vacation!" he proudly announced, referencing the company's adopted sales pitch. "They let us check them out to see how they work, so I thought I'd bring one along." We added it to the ever mounting pile of stuff.

Sometimes you have to bring just as much junk with you whether you are going away for a day or a month. Part of the reason for this was the fickle weather forecast. What does 40% chance of rain for four days straight mean, anyway? Will it rain over 40% of the county? Will it rain four minutes out of every ten? Did the meteorologists throw a dart that happened to land on 40%?

In other words, we had no idea how to dress or what to bring. The only solution in such cases is to bring it all. Long pants, shorts, short sleeves, and sweatshirts all crammed into our bag. Saddle up the bikes in case the weather is nice. We would hate to miss out on great trails if the sky was clear. On the other hand, bring the board games, the movies, and the recording equipment in case the adventures were limited to the indoors. And don't forget the one million books.

And the camera. Senator skimmed the instruction booklet for the camera that he had just purchased a few days before. He held it up to focus, threatening to take a picture of me in my junky house clothes, no makeup, and a sloppy ponytail. *I would seriously reconsider this action if I were you.* He got the hint. "Fine, I won't take your picture now, but you better be ready in Door County, because this thing comes everywhere with us now." *Drat! Foiled by my one-man paparazzi.*[*]

The next morning we started early, anxious enough to wake up before the alarm clock chimed. The sky was gray and

---

[*] Although, technically, that would make him paparazzo, the grammatical singular.

overcast, but no rain fell. This made an easy ride up, especially since we took the roads less traveled. By early afternoon we were riding the coast of Lake Michigan up along Door County's east side.

Somewhere near Jacksonport the fog rolled in. We slowed down, partly because of the increased tourism traffic and partly to avoid any potential deer that might decide to dart out from the mist. The trees and cottages took on an elfin look as the visibility dwindled significantly. Even so, we found the road we needed, and followed it past the weaver's shop* to the farmhouse where we would be staying.

We pulled into the driveway and got out of the car, stepping into a well organized mosquito attack. As I have probably mentioned before, Senator is a mosquito magnet. He could attract a sole mosquito from a mile away. Unfortunately, the entire summer had been mosquito-heavy, and the current damp, cloudy conditions in Door County made it prime flesh-eating season.

We did our best to shoo as we unpacked the car. Our friends Bill and Marge greeted us at the door, and I think we all started talking at once. There was the typical exchange of welcomes, the suggested plans for the next few days, and, of course, the rundown on the latest 1940s serials. "You've got *G-Men vs. The Black Dragon*, too?!" Bill asked excitedly.

"Yeah, I also just purchased *Undersea Kingdom* [featuring Lon Chaney, Jr.] , *Flash Gordon Conquers the Universe* [because, as Bond learned, the world is not enough], and *Zombies of the*

---

* Do weaver shops still exist, you may wonder? Apparently so, or at least one does in Door County. I have never paid much attention to said weaver shop (shoppe?) before, but amid the lush, green meadows and forest, it gave the area a decidedly medieval flavor. Perhaps I have underestimated the weaver shop. For all I know, it could be run by fairies, or better yet, an old crone. Either way, the shop seems to have survived the recession under King Barach I.

Stratosphere [need I say more?]. We also started *Radar Men From the Moon* at home. I gotta' get a flying suit like Commando Cody!" We continued to run through the entertainment options, to which Senator proudly added, "And I also have one million books with me."

Bill and Marge glanced at our car, puzzled. He then showed them the Nook. Throughout the week, we learned several key facts about Nook Loaner #2:

#1--It is not terribly comfortable to hold in one hand, unless your hand is large. This is highly inconvenient if you only have one hand, or if you ever plan to look cool while reading.

#2--While you can access electronic books already purchased/stored from anywhere, you can not shop for or purchase new books while away from your home wi-fi or 3G connection. So if are going to travel, you had better stock up before leaving.

#3--Reading an ereader screen is just plain annoying after a while. Is it as annoying as reading a computer screen? No. Is it more annoying than reading this book? In nine out of ten cases, yes.

#4--The battery lasts a long time. There, I've said something nice.

#5--It takes up less space than real books, especially if you have the touted one million books stored. (That's two nice things.)

#6--'Nook' is a very silly word that lends itself well to limitless junior high-maturity level jokes. Not that it stops me from making them every time Senator mentions the Nook.

#7--There are certain people for whom the Nook was lovingly created. We are not them.

Once we were settled in, Bill suggested we go for a ride to a bakery (always a good start). We piled into his car and headed out into the mist. Bill and Marge have come to Door County for about twenty years, and they had never seen it enveloped in fog. Bill actually mentioned this to a cashier at one point, and she looked at him in disbelief, mistaking his observation for inexperience with fog. Yes, Cashier Girl, we do actually have fog in Illinois. Never mind.

I forget which turn led us to the Dead End Socks. Somehow, though, we found ourselves slowly driving down a narrow, forbidden road. At the end of the road was a strict END OF ROAD TURN AROUND HERE sign, with a pair of mangled, once-white socks draped limply on an adjacent branch. One could only imagine what had happened to the unfortunate wearer of said socks. We decided not to explore further. If the socks at the edge of the woods did not get us, the mosquitoes surely would. Bill backed the car around and we departed the dark regions.

Back on the main road, we found the parking lot of the aptly named Door County Bakery. Beautiful perennial beds of many colors lined the front of the business, as they do throughout the area. I was dilly-dallying, admiring the flowers, when Bill realized the bakery was closed. It was the middle of the afternoon, but there was a sign explaining that they had run out of their signature Corsica loaf. Apparently that is how they determine their closing time each day. No problem. On to a backup bakery.

Grandma's Swedish Bakery was the next stop.* Inside the

---

* We completely ignored Grandma Tommy's bakery. I suppose it would have been fair to at least have a look inside, but the place suffers from some severe marketing flaws. For one, posted outside the building, larger than life, is one mean-ass looking cutout of the bakery's namesake. Clearly, she is not a grandma to be trifled with, which leads to the second curiosity-- the name. I have a Grandma cozy log building, which is attached to an inn, the first thing you notice is the pump organ. A card next to it explains that this solid looking antique was hauled across the ice one winter in the early 1900s. I, of course, was imagining how it would look in our home. Marge and Senator were quietly resisting the urge to play it, respecting the strict DO NOT TOUCH sign.

Turning left took us to the bakery itself. Cookies, pies, and Swedish sweets and treats galore lined the shelves. There were also dozens of jars of homemade lingonberry jam. *Hhmmm, this berry I do not know.* There was a small eating area, complete with lanterns and rustic tables and chairs, but we did not stay. Bill ordered a few fist-sized oatmeal cookies to go.

Our last stop of the afternoon was Al Johnson's. Yes, that's the place where the goats wander around munching grass on the roof, and the place that I always (incorrectly) want to call Al Jolson's. Amid the rain however, nothing was wandering or munching. Inside though, the place was buzzing with patrons and the traditionally costumed staff. The hostess sat us and we started to browse the menu.

I chose the traditional Swedish black bean burger. Okay, it was not exactly Scandinavian cuisine, but it sounded really tasty. Senator, on the other hand, went with the Swedish pancakes, a crepe-like wrap base with lingonberry sauce. Lingonberries, as it turns out, are a prized little red berry that are similar to a cranberry, but sweeter. Nine million Swedes can't be wrong. Delicious!

We enjoyed the rest of our meal and wandered into the gift shop. Sweaters, trinkets, and all things Swedish, (and a few things Norwegian) were packed into two small rooms. I couldn't help but notice a pair of Swedish flag socks on a rack. Perhaps there is an entire sock language of which we have no cultural

---

Dorothy and a Grandma Shirley. Betty, Annie, Rose, Julia, Florence-- all good choices, but Tommy???

knowledge.

The four of us do, however, know our classical music basics. As we waited outside the gift shop for Bill, we overheard a tourist ask about the instrumental music that was playing in the background. "Is that wedding music?" she inquired of the cashier.

We stifled our comments, but I am not sure I hid my rolling eyes. Bill couldn't take it. "That's Pachelbel's *Canon*," he explained politely, naming the renowned piece.

"Oh," the woman said flatly, clearly uninterested, and clearly convinced that, no, this was definitely the music she had heard at her cousin's wedding, and it did not sound anything like artillery.

Somehow, doing a lot of nothing wore me out. Back at the house, we visited and hung out, but when the guys decided to take a quick bike ride between rain showers, I declined the invitation. I was in for the night. Marge was with me, which gave us a chance to chat alone. In just a short time, we were deep into the subject of relationships. While we had endured some crummy ones, we are both aware of what a blessing it is to be with partners who reciprocate our love, effort, sense of humor, and strong commitment to enjoying life. I will always appreciate Marge's positive perspective and appropriate responses to a variety of situations.

Just as our talk was winding down, the men folk burst in. Their ride had energized them, and they were discussing deep topics of their own sort... like which serial we would watch over the next few nights. Oh, the options we had when it came to conquering evil in twelve to fifteen hair-raising episodes. It was unanimously decided: 1943's *G-Men vs. The Black Dragon*, which pitted the Allied good guys against a cruel Japanese saboteur ring. *I know who my money's on.*

Before fighting the Axis, however, it was game time. I often lament the dying art of the board game, but it seems to be experiencing a slight surge in interest. That is why I love the fact that there are still people who will spend vacation time gathered around a kitchen table, taking their dice, spinners, or tokens seriously. Between the four of us, we had enough games to stock a general store full of pickle-barrel sitters. Screw the Nook; we've got Yahtzee.

In fact, not only do we have Yahtzee, but we have Deluxe Yahtzee in the fancy zippered case, suitable for travel. I unzipped and tossed the dice onto the table. Once the official rules were established, the high roller began. Round and round we went, strategically retossing as necessary and filling in our score cards.

When it was all said and done, the big winner was... I forgot whom. But the big loser was definitely me, so I enthusiastically voted yes to a second game when Bill suggested we all play again. This time everyone had a better game; the dice were all warmed up now. This time when we tallied and announced each of our scores, I was... still dead last. It's hard to accuse the dice of being loaded when you are the one who brought them. Next year I'll have to bring Battleship.[*]

Now it was time for the featured attraction. We reserved our spots on the couches as Bill loaded up the dvd player. After ambitiously selecting "play all", the credits for *G-Men vs. The Black Dragon* began to roll in glorious black and white.[†] We settled in for World War II action that would have satisfied even the toughest nine-year old boy in 1943.

The G-Men (and one G-Woman) wasted no time in uncovering the fiendish plot of The Black Dragon society. Haruchi's gang had cleverly invented a delayed reaction flammable paint. When switched out with the U.S. Navy's real

---

[*] Senator can usually clobber me with his slick Yahtzee rolls, but the German in me can almost always sink his ships with few casualties to my navy.

[†] We watch so few modern releases that films in color are actually starting to look odd to me.

paint, ships would explode while out to sea. Now that is pure evil.

So just destroy the diabolical paint, you say? Sure, but what are you going to do when The Black Dragon figures out a way to blow up your towers? Or derails your trains? Or tortures your friends? Thank goodness Rex Bennett was on the job. His prowess for cracking heinous plots, combined with his superb ability to bail out of moving, burning, sinking, crashing, or exploding vehicles saw him through numerous chapters with titles like *Japanese Inquisition, Suicide Mission, Condemned Cargo,* and *Flaming Coffin.*

With so much action behind us, it was time for bed. The clock read 1:something or other. Senator and I said our good nights to Bill and Marge, and marched up the steep stairs to our room. Within ten minutes we were asleep to the sound of the drizzling rain.

The next morning, the smell of brewing coffee floated up the stairs to our room. Senator was asleep, but I was awake after a night of strange dreams and an even stranger stomach. I had indulged in too much vacation food, but coffee still sounded good. I slipped out of bed and got dressed. Senator turned over and sort of halfway woke up. "Did I keep you up?" I asked.

"Nomnm, sort of. You okay?" he slurred.

"Yeah, I guess I just ate too much. I've been eating pretty light at home. Too much change at once. I'm fine. No big deal."

"You should have gone into training for this... started eating pizza and junk for a few days before," he laughed, eyes still closed.

We made our way downstairs and joined Bill and Marge. I have determined that Bill sleeps very little while in Door County. He is always the last one to bed and the first one up. We fare pretty well on the deal since coffee magically appears each morning with zero effort on our part.

While we nibbled fruit and muffins, Marge began to

explain the plan for the day. "Do you guys like raw garlic cloves?" I choked on my pineapple. It was not a question I had anticipated at 8:00 in the morning. Senator, however, looked like a kid in a candy store... if all of the candy were made with garlic. His eyes lit up as Marge explained further. "There's this great market that has lots of homemade stuff, and they sell marinated garlic cloves..."

"Such a thing exists?!" interrupted Senator, with a wide, dopey grin on his face.

"They're really good. Margie, remember the time you almost ate an entire jar?" asked Bill. *Wow, and I thought we loved garlic.* Marge laughed and said she would not be eating quite that many cloves, but she maintained that they were a glorious delicacy.

Senator needed no convincing. "Marinated garlic? What are we waiting for?" With that, we cleaned up the kitchen and got ready for the day's first excursion. We were still hoping to squeeze a bike ride in, but so far the sky was not looking promising.

Once again Senator and I hopped into the back seat of Bill's car. We stopped at a few shops that were good for browsing, but finally we arrived at the magical purveyors of garlic. Though spotlighted by the anticipation, marinated garlic was not the only item on the shelves. Homemade pies, jellies, and various jars of things in liquid sat in neat rows on the shelves. Of course, local cherries were prominently featured. I could see this was going to require a basket.

I squeezed past a few browsing customers and grabbed a little hand basket. Now we could properly shop for our picnic. In the end, the four of us collected an odd assortment including the highly praised marinated garlic cloves, olives, jalapeno pickled brussels sprouts, rosemary bread, dried cherries (with sugar), dried cherries (without sugar), crackers, and peanut butter fudge. An unusual feast to be sure, but it was starting to sound more tempting than it did earlier that morning.

A short drive brought us to Cave Point Park. While the peninsula of Door County is only eighteen miles wide at its widest point, the temperature difference between the Green Bay coast and the Lake Michigan coast can vary significantly. The temperature had hovered around a very humid 80°F-82°F all morning, but at Cave Point, the wild winds whipped off the lake, chilling the air to the low 60s.

None of us had thought to bring jackets along, focusing instead on ways to stay cool. Oh well, we were there now, we had a gigantic picnic in tow, and the scenery looked liked something out of a novel set in Maine. We each loaded up with jars and boxes from the trunk. Bill chose a picnic table, and we huddled in pairs as we unpacked the spread.

At the center of the table, in its esteemed position, sat the jars (yes, two) of marinated garlic. We all sampled some, hoping, if nothing else, that maybe it would keep the mosquitoes away. It was tasty, and not as harsh as unmarinated raw garlic. It also made the dried cherries taste almost unbearably sweet. Yum!

I slapped at my leg. Contrary to its vampire-repelling reputation, the garlic did not ward off the miserable little blood suckers. We did notice that no one was walking too close to us, though. *If they only knew what they were missing*, I thought, as I bit off another hunk of bread.

When we had all had our fill of sour, sweet, bitter, and salty, we took the leftovers back to the car. Still shivering, we walked out toward the water. Because of the ever-present fog, there was no distinct horizon; the gray sky ran into the gray water. Out of the emptiness, big waves rolled in, one right after another. Senator had a small digital recorder with him, and he was able to capture the loud *crash-sler-oosh* as the waves slapped the rock and dispersed on the shore. This was my favorite moment on this trip. For just a while I could pretend (fairly convincingly) that we were in my beloved New England.

We watched the water for a while longer, and then returned to the car. Everything was suddenly quiet. You don't notice how loud and musical the waves are until you get away from them. There is so much energy in the Great Lakes. I don't think people who have never experienced them realize that they are really small, freshwater seas. In fact, all of that wonderful commotion had made me a little sleepy.

By the time we got back to the house, the clouds were breaking up a bit. Out came the sun, and gone was our chilly breeze off the lake. The pavement was wet and hot, but there was a window of opportunity for biking. Seizing our chance, we made a brief pit stop to reload the snacks, sunscreen, bug spray, and water bottles. Bill and Senator hooked the bikes up to their carriers on the backs of our cars, and we drove to Peninsula State Park.

Actually, I should say we drove to just outside of Peninsula State Park. Parking outside is free, but parking inside lets them snag you for $10 per car. Boooo. Either way the bike trail is easily accessible, so do as you will, Reader.

Once on the trail, I remembered why I had liked it so well from the last time we were there. There are just the right amount of hills and curves to keep it interesting, while still providing a decent workout. Most of the trail is in the shade, too, which was good since the chilly weather of Cave Point was already a distant memory. Single file, we followed Marge into the woods.

In five miles the ride takes you past a lighthouse to a popular beach. The water was filled with swimmers and loungers. Off to the side, brave souls played sand volleyball in the heat. Having drunk twice as much as usual, I was glad to see a convenience store that sold bottled water.

We parked our bikes and took a break for the second picnic of the day. Such decadence! Marge and I unpacked our portable snacks-- no jars of marinated garlic this round. Senator played with his new camera, and discovered a useful feature. By setting a timer and a rapid succession option, he was able to film Bill in ten frames, as he walked from the building to our picnic table. Now there's action for you. Imagine what fun we could have filming still shots of a serial-style fist fight in progress.

Before we got too comfortable or too tempted to nap, we remounted the bikes for the ride back. Again the trail was enjoyable, except for the stupid families. I don't mean to say that all families who ride bike trails are stupid; we just happened to encounter a few who were. For instance, why would you force children who are too small or too tired to pedal to parade along the trail, whining the entire way? *We WILL have fun and you WILL like it!*

Likewise, if you insist on towing a wide child-tote-cart-thing behind your bike, why do you feel the need to ride in the middle of the road? *No problem. We'll just go around you by riding over these jagged branches through this patch of poison ivy.* Then there was the I-Have-A-Bike-And-Therefore-I-Am-Entitled-To-Be-Here-So-No-Way-Am-I-Going-To-Let-You-Pass woman. The first time, I am cheerful and polite. "On your left," I call merrily. The second time, I am firmer, "On your left," I announce authoritatively. If you refuse to cooperate to our mutual benefit a third time, I simply yell, "Comin' through!" and barrel my way past. Senator has taught me well in this regard.

I was motivated to push myself hard, and I also wanted to escape The Families, so I zipped through the five return miles quickly. When I finally stopped, I guzzled the rest of my water bottle, in between wiping sweat and swatting mosquitoes. About five minutes later Marge emerged, also out of breath. Soon after, the boys came along, and we slowly rode out to the cars. It seemed like we were sweating water out as fast as we were drinking it in. I again thought of Cave Point, amazed that there was no happy medium in temperature.

It was a short drive to the house, and we quickly took our turns in the shower. Something about being clean makes me realize how tired I am. It is as though I can not fully relax when I am grimy or sweaty. Once the clean clothes are on and the wet hair is clipped up, though, I can easily melt on the closest couch.

Senator must have felt the same way. He started to read one of his million electronic books, and set it aside a few minutes later. He stretched out his legs and his head tucked its way onto my lap. I moved the book I was pretending to read, and readjusted my position. This was like the porch in Florida. This was my boy. This was good.

Eventually we each woke up groggily from our naps. I picked up my copy of *Liberty* by Garrison Keillor and read a few more pages. Bill and Marge worked through crossword puzzles, and Senator explored more of his camera. Though we were all in the same room, the rest of the afternoon passed quietly. Silent contentment is often underrated in the modern world, but it gives a person time to think. I was thinking about the upcoming school year, and how chaotic it would probably be at the beginning. Marge, on the other hand, had just begun a well-earned retirement. I hope she still continues to give me teaching advice...

When the thinking and the crosswording and the reading and the cameraing ebbed, we decided it was time for dinner. After the picnic feast, none of us expected to be hungry again, but we must have rode harder than we thought, because everyone had developed an appetite. The plan was to go out for Mexican food, to a restaurant that we had enjoyed the last time we were in town. In particular, we all remembered that Senator loved it, but he had no recollection of it whatsoever. Perhaps some cheese enchiladas would jar his memory.

We arrived at the restaurant and got out of the car to a hilarious spectacle. A complete nuclear family was dressed in matching rainbow tie-dyed shirts. They were not a family from the bike trail, but they could have been. On the kids, it was sort of cute. On Mom, it was pathetically fake-retro. On Dad, it was obviously a symbol of something that he had messed up royally, putting him in Mom's debt. "Bill, Marge, Senator-- I think we all know how we are dressing tomorrow..."

Inside the restaurant there was a twenty or thirty minute wait to get a table. Marge entered our party's name at the host stand, and we sat down in the miniscule waiting area. I had the pole position at the end of the L-shaped bench, next to some unsupervised kids. They flopped and kicked a few times, pushing each other off and giggling hysterically.

Okay, time for subtle crowd control. I very gracefully leaned over my legs, resting my chin on my hands, Audrey Hepburn-style. To Audrey's pose, however, I added a sharp left elbow, jutting out just far enough not to hit the kids, but for them to carelessly run into it the next time they dive bombed the bench. Within about twelve seconds, my plan worked. Back slammed the younger kid, surprising himself upon impact. I did not flinch, but continued to carry on my conversation with my friends. The funniest part was that the older kid then yelled at the younger kid for goofing off too much and running into me. Success! The lesson here: always keep your arms in shape... or at least your elbows.

As we remembered, the food at La Puerta was excellent. Senator still did not remember eating there, but he had no problem believing that he had enjoyed it. From the fresh garden salsa to the sizzling cheesy entrees, everything was perfectly prepared. I did not completely finish my meal because I was saving room for the dessert that waited back at the house. "Why not do both?" Senator observed.

I did not answer him. I was too busy looking out the window at the curious spectacle of a camouflaged child. All I could make out was a dad with a tie-dyed shirt holding something that had a head at one end and legs at the other. The rest of his tie-dyed son was hidden in there somewhere amid the rainbow swirls.

When we returned to the house I declared it fat pants time. Goodbye jeans; hello elastic waist vacation pajama bottoms.* We gathered around the table for the game of the night. 'Reminiscing' was given to me one Christmas by my parents, who know how much I love history and nostalgia, even if I wasn't around for most of the good stuff. To mix up generations, we decided to play guys against gals.

With each spin of the wheel, there were questions from a designated decade between the 1940s and the 1980s. Not surprisingly, as a group we scored better in the earlier years. Bill reigned superior in this game, usually adding knowledge above and beyond the required answer. That is part of the reason he is the perfect host, production engineer, and emcee of the 16mm Movie Club. Despite Marge's great stories when we landed on a 'reminiscing' square, the men still beat us badly. Still, I highly recommend this game for adult groups of mixed ages. You might even learn a thing or two about each other.

As was the established tradition, the night ended with dessert and a few chapters of *G-Men*. For this occasion, I had made a white chocolate and almond cheesecake with raspberry sauce, hence the fat pants. I swallowed the last spoonful of the creamy treat and set my plate in the sink. It was time to relocate to battle the Axis.

We were halfway through *G-Men,* and those Black Dragons were not letting up. One by one we dozed off to the sounds of fist fights, explosions, and a lot of tough talk. Leaving Rex Bennett in another lurch, we went to bed. I had absolutely no trouble sleeping this time.

Wednesday began with more drizzle. Anywhere there was lack of human activity, fog gathered. Marge flipped on the local news for the weather forecast. Once we got past the inane pleasantries of the news anchors, the radar map came up. It

---

* suitable for cramming in an extra 1,000 calories per day.

looked like the real rain would hold off until the afternoon. If we got moving now, we could possibly take the planned trip to Washington Island to ride the bikes.

Bill manned the waffle maker while we discussed the strategy. "Well, we can take the ferry to the island, and if it isn't raining, we'll ride to the beach. We'll just play it by ear," proposed Marge. That sounded good to us. So what if it didn't work out? It wasn't like we had other pressing plans. If only all of life were that laid back.

We drove north across the peninsula toward the ferry port. A few miles before we reached it, the fog increased heavily.[*] If it was this thick on the mainland, I assumed the island would have next to no visibility. This would rule out a bike ride, as we would have to share the road with cars. Oh well, at least we would get a boat ride out of the deal.

The fog was thicker still at Northport. Undeterred, Marge and I bought ferry tickets while Bill and Senator parked. There was zero visibility beyond the dock itself. We could not even see if there was a boat attached to the other end. Again, sky blended in to sea.

That did not stop the Segway riders, though. From out of the mist, like aliens too lazy to walk or pedal, arose the motorized group of stoic dorks. They coolly rode over the hump of the ramp, fanny packs securely in place. Just like the last time the four of us encountered a gang of Segwayists, we made no attempt to hide our laughter. And that was even before seeing the Leader, who had a stick figure Segway rider on the back of his tee shirt.

The crossing was a strange sensation. We were on a ferry

---

[*] One sign I could read, despite the fog, was an advertisement for homemade goods. This is common in Door County, except that they don't usually spell it "ho-made" like this sign did. Perhaps it is a job training center for ex-prostitutes?

deck, along with a few dozen others, but we were isolated from the rest of the world. At least it looked that way. There was nothing but 360° of gray enveloping our boat.* The sensation could be described as flying through clouds in slow motion, while standing outside of the airplane.

When you have half an hour to kill and not much scenery to view, you tend to focus your attention on people watching. There was a couple, some families, a few senior citizens, and The Group. The Group-- though earning points for bringing actual bicycles, rather than Segways-- lost points in the accessory category. I am not talking about belts, purses, and hats; I mean accessories that no human should possess, at least until the robots take over.

The most vocal of The Group's females had something sticking out of her head. Being inclined to mercy toward the unfortunate, I believed the telescopic device to be a medical necessity. I even thought it admirable that she was not letting the contraption stand in the way of her enjoyment of the great outdoors. Silently, I wished her a pleasant day.

Then I realized what the protruding object was. Granted, rear view mirrors can come in very handy when biking. Many people attach them to their bikes for added safety and visual scope. I have never seen someone attach one to her head, though. If one chose to wear one's rear view mirror, however, I would think it far more comfortable (and more conducive to conversation) if one collapsed the object until needed. Not this woman-- rear view mirror fully extended, ready at a second's notice to spot any danger which may have lurked behind her. I probably should not criticize it, though. Al Qaeda won't be sneaking up on her anytime soon.

Soon we approached the dock at Washington Island to see a strange sensation. The sky was completely clear and sunny.

---

* Senator has a recording of the fog horn to prove it.

The Segways didn't look so magical now. There was no problem with visibility, so we jumped on our bikes and took off.

We rode past farms and a few small businesses. At one point the air was perfumed with a field of golden flowers. Across another field horses sauntered around carelessly. A cool, breezy coast led us to Schoolhouse Beach.

By this time we were pros at picnicking. We parked our bikes between the trees and opened plenty of snacks. The air was warm again, and the water beyond the rocky beach looked inviting. We did not go in, but a group of young boys could not resist. Overheard as Dad struggled with the Responsible Kid to blow up the inflatable boat: "Are they in the wa-- nobody better be in the water yet!" Too late, Dad. The rest of the bunch was already submerged and engaged in a serious water fight. I am sorry we could not join them.

It was time for the Schoolhouse Bitches[*] and their men to leave Schoolhouse Beach. We dug in, pedaling slowly up the steep hill that led back to the main road. Traffic had picked up somewhat, but it was still negligible. Marge led our pack until we stopped at the Albatross.

The Albatross is always busy. As the island's number one ice cream and junk food hot spot, it makes a great stopover on the way back to the ferry. Part of the draw is their huge menu. Unless you are looking for a marinated garlic sundae[†], they probably stock your desired flavor and ingredients. I was immediately charmed by the coffee malt, and talked Senator into the same. Had I known they only come in one size, and that size is huge, we could have split one.

We finished our ride and loaded the bikes onto the ferry. Clouds were starting to form over the island, but it was still

---

[*] Bill's affectionate term for educator pals Marge and Wendy.

[†] Although, they might be able to work something out for you if you asked.

clearer than the gray lake. Just as when we had crossed to the island, the fog kept everything hidden. Once again, the Segwayists boarded. Now there were only three. They had started out with several more. You can fill in the details here, Reader. Perhaps the Dead End Socks had something to do with their disappearance. Perhaps we'll never know.

On the way back to the house, Bill and Marge wanted to try the Door County Bakery again. This time it was open. Inside, the aroma of freshly baked bread permeated the place. An open doorway led to the bakery in back. As I was craning my neck to see the bakers at work, a lady came out carrying a large wooden board with a Corsica loaf on it. This signature version of French bread with olive oil and sesame seeds weighs over five pounds, all of which could easily be consumed by me if left alone with it for a few hours. Good bread is truly a divine gift.

The rest of the store held many other specialties in the vein of pastas, deli goods, and olives. There was even a small coffee bar. It would have been tempting to sit down and have a cup, but the place was instantly filling up. We assumed that a tour bus had pulled in, but it was just a rush of people waiting to buy their favorite breads. The old fashioned 'take a number' system was still in place, and the plastic cards were getting a workout. Once Marge had her Corsica loaf, we pardoned our way past the crowd to the door.

Again I was grateful for some afternoon relaxation time. The bike ride was not as strenuous as the day before, but plopping on the couch felt just as good. It was hard to believe this was already our last night there. I looked out the window to the back yard. Normally during the summer, birds swarm at the feeders, devouring pounds of birdseed like they were at a Roman feast. So far we had only seen one blue jay hopping around the ground picking up a few stray seeds. The constant fog and drizzle had even thrown the birds off.

Later that evening, we went out for pizza. Though not a beer drinker, this is where I learned that Wisconsin exclusively sells a beer called Spotted Cow. The name is locally appropriate given the amount of farms in Wisconsin, but to me it suggested that milk was added to the beer. At least I can add it to the list of craft brews I have heard of. That ought to impress 'em at The Sugar Maple.

Naturally, after eating too much pizza, one needs a dessert of some sort. The cheesecake was long gone, but fortunately for us, Yum Yum Tree was nearby. I seemed to remember a mall store by the same name when I was a kid, but this was a *true* candy store. We stepped inside and argued about the familiar aroma. Toffee? Caramel? I declared it to be the scent of the leftover melted butter after one removes the cooled cookies from a baking sheet.

The first job was just to narrow down the categories. The ice cream counter was not a draw, as I am not a huge fan. Hard candy has never been a temptation, so there was no need to go to that wall of bins. Vanilla fudge, on the other hand, had distinct possibilities. "Did you see these?" asked Senator, knowing his girlfriend all too well. *What's this?* I forgot about the fudge for the moment and immediately plunked down my cash for the essential item that no fun store should be without-- a rubber chicken key chain. As if that were not enough to make a Yum Yum Tree excursion complete, I found out that the rubber chicken lays a rubber egg as well.

We got back into the car and rolled along Highway F back to the house. The time for the rumored podcast was now upon us. This was Bill's baby, an idea that had been rattling around in his mind for at least two years. He and Senator would venture out to the garage to record half an hour of unscripted commentary on the current vacation. Marge and I remained in the house, temporarily isolated from the magic. When the session ended, though, they hooked up the stereo system to share the fruits of their labor.

From the onset, they had established a solid yet natural dynamic for their roles. Bill was the front man, telling entertaining stories, and Senator was the background sidekick guy. The subject matter of the first episode of *On the Lam* centered around an event that took place while caravaning to Washington Island. As we were driving through a town slowly, an oblivious family stood on the side of the road, debating the use of the crosswalk.

When no one chose to use it, Bill proceeded. Then a boy sort of started to step into the crosswalk. Bill stopped, the boy looked totally confused, and *then* his useless parents, who heretofore had been too busy gazing over the sea of restaurants and shops to pay attention to their son, decided to join the kid in the crosswalk, loosely arranged between either side of the street. The best part was when the guy, khakis still perfectly creased and hair still well-coiffed, looked at Senator and I with a "do-you-believe-this-guy?" shrug, referring to Bill, who had been forced to hit the brakes due to their negligence. Sorry, Buddy. We're with them, are you are the reason local businesses love the tourism but hate the tourist.

On the Lam #1 was a success. Next it was on to the Yahtzee rematch. Two nights ago I had been shamed as the double mega loser. This night was my revenge. The dice were my friends. I practically called my rolls as though I was a pool shark naming the pockets. I easily won my way through both rounds, evening out my week, and securing my position as an average Yahtzee player-- yes!

I don't need to tell you how our evening concluded, Reader. You have probably guessed by now that it involved sweets and good old patriotic punching in black and white. Bill watched several chapters, and I think Senator made it through most of them. Marge and I, on the other hand, had no ambitions of staying up. We secured our pillows, kicked our legs up on our respective gentlemen's laps, and promptly fell asleep. Good night, Rex.

I was actually happy that it was still drizzling Thursday morning when we woke up. It is too much of a slap in the face when, after raining throughout a vacation, the sun comes out to gloat while you are packing to leave. I looked at the pile of clothes lying near, on top of, and in our travel bag. No point in dealing with that right away. We went downstairs to join Bill and Marge for coffee and waffles.

Of course, by coffee and waffles I mean coffee, waffles, watermelon, cherries, muffins, and whatever else was displayed on the big kitchen table. The picture window to the back yard was still devoid of birds. Maybe we should have just hung up mosquito feeders. There were still plenty of those around. We visited for about an hour, discussing all that we had done in the past few days and different events that we would like to plan in the fall. Soon it was time to pack up.

In less than an hour, we were ready to go. We hugged our goodbyes and swatted a few last Door County mosquitoes. The car was stuffed and so were we. In fact, we already had plans to live solely on watermelon for the next day or two just to allow our bodies to recuperate from the vacation grazing.

Senator drove as I navigated us out through the meadows and onto the main roads. We chatted for a while, and then I fell asleep. This pattern continued on and off into Illinois. I do not recall seeing a WELCOME TO ILLINOIS sign, but I was awake for the THANK YOU FOR USING THE ILLINOIS TOLLWAY beacon.

We traveled along quietly until I remembered that Senator had not yet decided how he would spend his following day off. "Did you decide if you're going tomorrow night," I asked. Several weeks before, he had been invited to a reunion for a club that he used to d.j. for, back when he was too young to be entering a club, let alone working at one. Wednesday Punk

Night became quite the popular success in Joliet, Illinois, but Dave Rave was back in the d.j. booth, far more interested in the great punk and new wave records than the people on the dance floor.

"No, I'm not going. I really didn't even know those people. I never saw anyone. I did a pretty good job of staying hidden," he explained. In my gut I felt that we should go, but it was his deal, so I was fine with a night at home instead. After all, how often did we get the luxury of an entire day off together after a vacation?

By mid-afternoon we were home. As we lugged our gear into the back door, we heard the expected beeping of our answering machine. At the first opportunity, I played back the messages, mainly to stop the irritating bleep. Of six messages, four were personal invitations for Dave Rave to come to the reunion. Each talked about what a key part he played in bringing the best music, and how much they would love to have him attend. The last message ran out the time limit on our machine. He shrugged and grinned at me. "I guess we're going..." Good. With that, he picked up the phone while walking over to the record cabinet to explore.

Chapter 5
Victorian Mosquitoes: Late July 2010

The original plan, essentially, was insane. After recording a three day, seven set jazz festival, we would have one day (spent at work, in Senator's case) before leaving for a marathon road trip. The drive out would take about thirty-three hours. For one brief day we would stay put, enjoying the full splendor of the redwood forest in northern California. Then, lest we get too comfortable, we would leave bright and early to begin the long journey home. Once home, I would have one day to throw together the beginning of the semester, which I had neglected to do in the spring, since I had left school thinking I would not have a job. Senator would return home to face approximately 100 hours of mixing the material he had recorded just before leaving. *Whose ridiculous idea was this?*

In truth, it was mine. Back in April, it sounded great on paper, giving me something to look forward to as I determined my next career move. In May, it looked challenging, but still doable. By June, as I considered the whole matter one day while washing my hair-- epiphanies always occur in the shower for me-- I declared it the worst plan for a vacation I had ever made.

I knew exactly how those sixty-six hours in the car would

play out. Two people would sit, exhausted, side-by-side, each silently pondering the mountain of work that awaited at home. Naturally, this would make us more likely to be irritable, and less likely to appreciate the grandeur of the open road. What if we kept the time off, but worked on our projects at home, and just got away for three days? When I presented my plan to Senator, he seemed relieved. I knew I had made the right choice when I realized that I wasn't even bothered by the fact that it would be another year until we added a new state to our list of those visited.

That is how our thirty-three hour journey to the northwest coast of the United States turned into a three hour journey to the northwest coast of Illinois. Galena, a small town whose history and clever marketing have capitalized on its 'quaintness' (almost to a fault), had been on the list for quite some time. Years ago I had visited Galena, and I remembered the picturesque river setting, dotted with beautifully restored Victorian homes and their immaculate gardens. Since then, I had really absorbed the small town spirit, and I imagined sharing a lazy coffee date with Senator at an old-fashioned café. We would not be rushed, and we would even have the satisfaction of knowing that some of our work at home was caught up.

There were also plenty of local parks. If we could balance sweaty summer outdoor activities like hiking and boating with the pampering of a bed and breakfast, it would be a perfect three day getaway. I dove into the process of narrowing down accommodations. By the time I tossed out any inn that allowed smoking, children, or pets, my list had been whittled down from dozens to just four. Reasoning that two nights at an upscale b&b is still cheaper than a week on the road, I splurged on a third floor room that included a double soaking tub.

The last Thursday in July was hot. Of course it was, you say. It was very humid, too. What did we expect? The difference was that it followed obediently in a line of about three months of hot, humid misery. In 2010, Illinois experienced one of its hottest summers on record, and certainly the hottest in my lifetime. It was not altogether unexpected, though. After all, the piper had to be paid for the gorgeous, dry, cool summer of 2009. *I knew it was too good to last!* So with plenty of water and sunscreen, we left for the first stop on the way to Galena.

Like anywhere in Illinois, summer means construction. Other states experience a greening of the world during this season; we detect a particular neon-oranging. Even though we avoided most major roads, the familiar barrels, lane closures, and detours were abundant. Still, we were patient. It was our vacation, and on vacation I do not let a slight change in plans stress me out.

That is, until I find out that I have driven thirty minutes out of my way and made various unnecessary turns, all because no one thought to place a detour sign where it was most needed. This was the case in Nowhere, Illinois[*]. I double and triple checked my route, and even made the novice mistake of ignoring my gut feeling, in the erroneous belief that the road would be marked accurately. *Surely there would be a sign if I was being rerouted, so I had better just continue this way.* Not so. In the end, I relied on my own sense of direction to get us to roughly where we needed to be, which, in fact, was on a road that we were on in the first place. One stupid sign, if properly placed, would have informed me that I could have simply stayed on the road and bypassed all of the suckers who fell for the detour.

Eventually we arrived at Mississippi Palisades State Park. Following the roads into the park leads you up to heights that overlook the mighty Mississippi River. My plan was to hike a mile or so up through the woods and enjoy a light lunch with a scenic view. We were prepared for the basics of the situation, but there was no way we could prepare for the onslaught of

---

* not actual name, but might as well be

hungry mosquitoes. Not five minutes along the trail the little demons surrounded us. I think I even heard a few of them laughing at my feeble organic botanical bug spray. *Essential plant oils-- is that all you got?!*

Needless to say, the hike was a short one. It lasted about as long as it took to jog back down the hill and out of the woods. Once in the sun, we were fairly safe, so I hatched plan B. We needed some form of exercise, so maybe we could at least take a walk through the campground. It was not ideal, but it would give us a chance to stretch our legs.

On a hot Thursday morning, not much is going on in a campground. We dutifully followed the pavement that ran along the various sections of the park. A few tenters and r.v.ers hung out at their campsites, but there was not much in the way of scenery. The backdrop was a pretty forest, and along the opposite side was a patch of land devoted to native prairie plant species, but that was about it. The butterflies seemed happy though, so I guess it was doing whatever native prairie is supposed to do. However, when we turned back to see a large woman yapping on her cell phone loud enough for even the butterflies to hear[*], we took it as our cue to head back to the car.

We sat in the car and ate our little lunch of crackers and fruit. We were trying to be 'good' in anticipation of the treats that we planned to enjoy once in Galena. It would have been nice to at least drive through the park while nibbling, but the main scenic road was closed for-- you guessed it-- construction. Maybe we will come back some day in the colder weather, but summer just isn't the season to visit state parks.

The next spot for an attempted hike was Caspar Bluff. Unlike large state parks, with their well developed parking lots, roads, and trails, Caspar Bluff is the result of a land and water

---

[*] No, Virginia, butterflies do not have ears. In rare cases, humans have been known to envy this trait.

reserve effort by a group of Galena area locals. When you turn off the road to its 'entrance', it looks like you are driving through a farmer's side yard, into his meadow. As no pitchforked landowners came running after us, we continued.

There was a small lot that held a handful of cars, but beyond that, a single clear path led to an open expanse of prairie. We walked the ¼ mile or so to the high point. From there you could continue down the slope into a loose group of old oak trees, or you could sit at a strangely solitary picnic table and enjoy the view of the Mississippi River below. We chose the picnic table.

Here, too, butterflies flitted everywhere. It was very quiet, except for the sounds one expects to hear in nature. Nothing humanly created, though. We talked for a few minutes and then sat silently again. A warm, wet breeze whipped around the hilltop. It was very peaceful, but like everywhere else in Illinois, very hot and humid. The weather was knocking us out, so we trudged back to the air conditioned car once more.

There was still plenty of time to kill before we could check-in to our room, so we drove to Galena and then east, to the small(er) town of Elizabeth.* Elizabeth is famous (in minute historical circles) for being the site of the Apple River Fort.

---

* Heading north into Galena means taking Blackjack Road. The road is convenient in terms of location, but it includes many hills and curves, making it difficult to zip along carelessly. This is fine if you are on vacation and appreciative of the rural sites. Locals, however, have no patience for this. They zoom past, nearly dumping themselves off the roadside in some instances. If you do not get out of their way, they ride your tail until the first hint of opportunity, and then fly by you, never minding the fact that they could not begin to guess if the oncoming lane is clear for passing. This was the sentiment every time we had occasion to use this road over the course of the weekend. Appropriately, Senator dubbed it "Jackass Road".

When we accidentally missed the entrance to the visitor center, though, we saw interesting sites of another sort. Farms all around the town looked oddly ragged. We soon realized why.

Once we had settled on a vacation in Galena, it was no surprise that less than a week before we arrived, severe storms had dumped record amounts of rain onto the land. Throughout the area, crops were damaged or destroyed as rivers rose, drenching fields. When the water finally receded, cornstalks were left caked with mud and debris. In low lying areas, the water line was well over a tall adult's head. Evidence that Senator and Wendy were coming to town was all over. *From Katrina to Galena.... *sigh*.*

The visitor center at the Apple River Fort was ice cold. Wonderful! An enthusiastic guide greeted us and explained that a small band of about seventy settlers had heard that Chief Black Hawk and his band of warriors were coming through, so they slapped up a small fort for protection.* Generally it was the men's duty to defend the community, and the women's duty to hunker down and pray and cry and such. Being outnumbered in manpower by more than 2:1, however, a few courageous women realized that they would have to pitch in big time if they were going to save themselves from Black Hawk's band. They rallied the others and worked nonstop to steadily supply the men with ammunition to keep up the defensive fire.

Thinking there must be more men in the fort than he had calculated, Black Hawk called off the attack. Of course, it was not a total loss for him; he raided the pioneer cabins that were outside the fort, yielding goods and probably food. He stopped short of burning down the cabins though. The smoke might have given his position away to the federal government, who by this time was pursuing him throughout the countryside.

Or so the story goes. As for the town's name, supposedly

---

*about the size of a single residential city lot

it was the brave Elizabeth who first determined that the women needed to assist in their own defense at the fort. Whom Elizabeth actually was, we were informed, has been a source of some contention for the better part of the last hundred years. Many descendents of the 'true Elizabeth' claim genealogical ties to the town's name, but records are sketchy at best.

At any rate, we walked up the path to the reproduction fort, which stands at the original site. It was worth seeing, but we did not spend too much time there, either. By this time the sun was sweltering, and we decided that the 'work' part of the vacation was over. There was just enough time to drive back to Galena and sip an iced coffee before check-in.

As I have stated, a serene coffee date was one of the priorities of the weekend. I had envisioned it for the past month. In 2003, I met Senator while working at a bookstore where the aroma of freshly brewed coffee was a constant backdrop to our many, many conversations. Since then, we have enjoyed countless cups together, sometimes in a busy café, sometimes in front of the stereo speakers at home, and sometimes in total silence. Now we found ourselves walking Main Street in Galena, in search of a decent java spot.

There are surprisingly few coffee shops in Galena's six blocks or so of tourist trap-- merely two by our count. We stepped into an old storefront that led to an urban/modern/chic café with some tables and an area set up like a living room. The room was pleasant, but the coffee was odd. My best attempt at a description would be "warmed-over, thinned-out, coffee-flavored syrup remains". Coffee it was not, and we have our own theory as to why.

Clearly, this joint was a front for an organization that had nothing to do with dispensing caffeinated beverages. First of all, the baristas[*] looked like Cuban communist nationals. Their classic Caribbean good looks and Fidel-style military garb did not connote espresso beans and steamed milk. Then there was the back room. While all food or beverage establishments have a back room that serves as a storeroom/kitchen area, such rooms are generally only about the size of an average bedroom. Often, there is not even a door separating such rooms from the counter area. The back room in this café, however, was large and definitely closed off. Who knows what nefarious activities took place behind the solid, windowless door? Finally, there was the fact that they made a shitty cup of coffee. Any business-- especially one that fronts as a café-- ought to be able to at least brew an acceptable pot of Folgers.

We dumped the remainder of our so-called coffee and walked outside. We noticed that the crowd on the street was heavily female. During the past decade, Galena has worked hard to become a girls' weekend destination. This is a concept that eludes me. If I'm going to stroll along historical streets, pay too much for dinner, and stay in a town known for its romantic inns, I sure as heck am not taking girls with me. I am bringing Senator, and we are not going to be braiding each other's hair... although, I suppose we could.

We wound our way to the car and drove less than a mile to our bed and breakfast. Inside, we were greeted warmly by the innkeeper, who led us through Civil War era rooms filled with antiques. Fellow guests sat on a sofa in the parlour, taking turns

---

[*] *Baristi* is only used as the plural form of barista in Italian, or in cases where the servers are especially trained in the art of coffee preparation. (These were definitely baristas.)

gazing through a stereoscope.* We continued up the sturdy wooden staircase to our third floor room. The window overlooked the side yard of a neighboring mansion. The focal point of the mauve room was the soaking tub, and the bathroom was immaculate. It seemed perfect. I just had one question: "Do you allow photography throughout the house?" I asked our hostess.

Once permission was secured, Senator plopped our second suitcase onto the chair. Years ago, I used to give tours at a Victorian mansion in Naperville, Illinois. Even though it was volunteer work, and I was not being paid, the historian in me insisted on the authenticity of my costume. Since I could not find a proper vintage dress, I commissioned the sewing of a replica 1894 formal day dress, befitting a lady of stature. I managed to spend about ten times more on that dress than any of my other dresses, yet, I had no photos of myself in the dress.

This setting would change that. Finally I had the perfect backdrop for a number of shots that would logically do the dress justice. It was late afternoon as I assembled my outfit, layer upon layer. *Thank God for the Victorian window air conditioner!* Once the hat was secured in place, I scooped up my skirts and Senator grabbed his camera.

Thankfully, no one else was around as we trudged through the home, executing our amateur photo shoot. I posed on the couch, and then standing against the fireplace. Lace curtains filled the background of another shot. When I came across a messy desk full of antique items, I used the props for the camera's benefit. Then we moved the party to the garden. I gave my best impression of wistfulness (because it seemed like a

---

* This original inspiration for the Viewmaster is a hand-held set of lenses that surrounds the eyes, blocking out side light and focusing on a pair of photographs. The photographs are identical, except for their angles and depth of field. When viewed together, one's eyes naturally combine them into a three-dimensional image.

Victorian thing to do), careful not to smile as the stone fountain statue stared back at me. When we had exhausted nostalgia, we ducked back into the house and up to our room. Jeans and a t-shirt felt pretty darn good.

The experience is significant in that I am generally terrified of cameras.* Senator has been on a diligent campaign to convert me to a willing subject, but I do not like being a focal point unless I am in character. I could be very comfortable acting on stage or screen, but ask Wendy to smile for a quick snapshot and I instantly get nervous. Although, I must be making progress since I no longer shake and sweat when surprised by a camera.

By this time we were hungry, so we left the house to walk downtown. Surprisingly, there were not many options for mid-range eateries. You could find a few upscale restaurants, but we needed something more relaxing and casual. On the other hand, we had no interest in the noisy, sporty bar scene. Eventually, against our intentions, we ended up at a pizza place. This was partly due to getting more tired and hungry with every block, and partly due to the advertised "double decker pizza". *Well that can't be all bad.*

Procento's crammed too many tables into too small of a space, with a noisy overhead television at one end of the room. I mentally gave it a 2 for ambiance, as I stared directly into Senator's eyes to avoid the peripheral view of couples who were dining too close for comfort on either side of us. Just then, Senator pointed out a positive sign. "I think that's the pizza maker," he said, indicating a white-haired, grinning man in the

---

* This is nothing new. In fact, my siblings laugh when comparing our school pictures because they are all smiling, with their generous dimples glowing, while I look like the cameraman had just threatened to beat me. I have my revenge, though. Now I work at a school, and every year I refuse to have my picture taken for the yearbook. Take that, establishment.

back.

I glanced-- but not too obviously, lest our neighbors think I was craning my neck for a bite of their pie-- at the open kitchen. Sure enough, a very friendly man who clearly enjoyed his life's calling was slipping pizzas in and out of a brick oven. The room smelled wonderful. In fact, the delicious aroma of garlic and tomatoes just about drove us mad as we endured the slow service. Eventually dinner arrived, and it was well worth the wait. There are many ways to make a successful pizza, but the brick oven was born for the 'za. Mmmmmm....

I did not want to overplan our getaway, so I figured that after dinner we would just walk around town, perhaps ducking into any venues that had interesting music or art. This did not go as expected, though. By 8:30pm, it seemed that the downtown was closed, save for a few bars. We were reminded of the time we assumed lower Manhattan would be hopping on a Sunday evening. Not so.

No big deal. We had a considerable walk back to the b&b, and by that time we would be ready to sit anyway. Better yet, sit and soak. As soon as we entered our room, I kicked my shoes off and started filling the massive tub. Yes, we are conservative when it comes to utilities at home, but on vacation, I have no problem using more gallons of water for one bath than I normally do for four showers. Likewise, I carelessly reject towels after using them only once.

So when you spent a hot summer day in activities as varied as hiking, visiting a historical site, holding a photo shoot, perusing a downtown, and enjoying a soothing tubby, how do you fittingly conclude it? With a VH1 1980s one-hit wonders countdown, of course. Light from the mansion next door shone through our window, while light from the television flickered. Has-been celebrities took turns recalling the decade of decadence, and I think I dozed off to a keyboard-laden A Flock of Seagulls.

The best weather of the week was predicted for Friday. This was encouraging as it was our only full day in Galena. That, of course, was in theory. By Friday morning, the forecast called for rain mixed with drizzle. *Well that rules out the garden tour and picnic I was going to surprise Senator with.* Missing a meal was hardly an issue, though. We got ready and wandered down to the twin dining rooms for breakfast. The coffee was ready, and our hostess was eager for us to try her French toast with fresh summer fruit. She even served us cheese instead of the sausage that the others ate.

Along with the good food at a bed and breakfast comes casual conversation with other guests. Most, like us, were on short vacations. Unlike us, they usually sought a break from kids. It is always funny to see people's reactions to us in situations like this. We probably look more like we should be on tour with a band than staying at a historical inn. People also tend to assume we are younger than we are. They make comments like, "someday when you have kids," exchanging what they believe is an inside joke among the *real* adults at the table. With those presumptions, people don't always know how to take us. They expect a couple of punks out for novelty, but they are sometimes surprised that we can hold actual conversations on history, music, travel, psychology, or world affairs. Stereotypes are almost as much fun as stereoscopes...

After breakfast we ventured out into the drizzle, back to Main Street. Despite the "0%" chance of rain that continued steadily, there was a sizable crowd of tourists and escapist-housewives. Many of the shops catered to these types, decking out their displays in pink accoutrements and wine paraphernalia. Some items even sported anti-male witticisms. Lame.

There were two shops that we did enjoy, however. The first was a candy/junk store that catered primarily to Baby Boomers, with a few Gen-X items thrown in for good measure. They sold all of the old-fashioned candy that people used to give at Halloween, back when it was fun and completely uncensored by overprotective parents. From candy cigarettes to wax pop bottles, all naughty habits could be freely encouraged in the average six-year old. Then there was the gag section. How could any red-blooded American kid grow up without a fake ice cube containing a fake fly, or a pile of rubber dog crap? If you were really lucky, or maybe had a rich aunt, you could take home the antique Radio Flyer wagon that sat untouched in the upper level.

After enjoying the edible museum, we dialed up the culture a bit and went to the Fine Books store. I do not remember the name of it, but that is what the sign outside read. There, beautiful rare editions by authors known and unknown lined the shelves. The real gems were encased under glass, which is where we discovered an 1893 book that contained notes from the committee meetings that planned the World's Columbian Exposition of that year.

We followed the staircase upward to a second level. Classical music played softly in the background, and I could see the rain running down the narrow windows. This would be a wonderful spot to have a cup of coffee. Stupid communist café.

Just then, Senator pointed out the strangest piece of the shop's collection. He held what looked to be a 1970s version of a Sherlock Holmes board game. I assume it was some ripoff of Clue, but you had to love the playing board, which showed a dated post-British Invasion Sherlock hot on the trail of a shaggy Professor Moriarty. The groovy game is afoot, Watson!

We left Fine Books and wandered a bit more until we were hungry. When on vacation, we have come to love the cheese-and-olive-based lunch. We can usually find a specialty shop that sells these basics, albeit overpriced, along with other odds and ends that pair well. In Galena there is such a shop, which also sells olive oils from around the world. The oil was tempting, but we selected crackers, olives, cheese (creamy), cheese (stinky), and a giant pickle to top it all off. Carrying our brown bag of delicacies, we entered the curtain of drizzle once more to walk back to our room. This picnic would take place indoors, where the temperature was about fifteen degrees cooler, and the humidity was about 60% more tolerable.

Once we had stuffed ourselves full of imported, tasty snacks, it did not take long to doze off. It was a hardcore nap-- the kind where you sleep deeply, dream heavily, and wake up with no idea what time of day (night?) it might be. We had not worked very hard, so I don't know why we were so tired. Sometimes I think your body just knows when it has permission to check out for a while. Our jobs and projects were left at home, so there was nothing to do but force ourselves to relax.

Of course, after such a long snooze, one needs to rejoin the world of the conscious. As on other trips, one of my favorite ways to do this is to bust out the Yahtzee. Naturally, Senator beat me. I should suggest that we start playing for money... as long as I am allowed to bet against myself.

We were ready to get out of our room again, but the rain was heavier, limiting our options. For some reason I thought of driving to Dubuque. The Mississippi River and Iowa border was less than twenty miles away, and it seemed like we should at least ride through the edge of another state, given that the original plan was to drive to California. So, we hopped in the car and drove to Iowa. The End.

Actually, we road out past town, through some rolling farmland. Then it really started to pour, limiting visibility. The windows fogged up and we adjusted knobs until the outside and inside of the windows were clear enough to see the road. Not long afterward, we crossed the big bridge, kissed at the state line, and drove around the block to get back on the Illinois-bound side. It was anticlimactic, but at least it killed some time, and it did not involve a television or computer.

It was nearing 8:00pm, so we decided that if we wanted

dinner, we had better find somewhere before the town rolled up the sidewalks for the night. It was already starting to look abandoned, even though it was a weekend. We cruised the main drag again, noticing nothing of particular interest. At the far end of the strip, we parked the car. Maybe we would have better luck finding something on foot.

Seven blocks later, at the exact opposite end of the downtown, we found a cozy and rustic restaurant. Had we seen this earlier, we could have saved ourselves time and steps. Ironically, the restaurant was closer to our inn than it was to our car. *Feels like being in Chicago.*

Boone's was a perfect choice, even though it was the only choice. We had a booth to ourselves, with no one seated at the nearby tables. In the background, we could hear a few locals visiting and goofing around. We listened in as we waited for our food. "...Then I had to rescue some drunk-ass tourist in a rental canoe, lost on the river..." It was hilarious! The 20-something year old guy went on to complain about tourists who overestimate their outdoorsy prowess once they have had a few too many drinks. One minute they are browsing the shops; the next minute they are floating down the Galena River with no sense of direction or skill.[*]

Our food arrived hot and delicious. The generous, sloppy sandwiches were piled high with grilled vegetables. Our server was pleasant, too. She seemed genuinely bothered by the fact that we would have to walk back in the rain. Rethinking the matter, perhaps we *were* to be pitied. We agreed that we had better order a piece of raspberry cheesecake to split.

By 9:30pm, Galena was a ghost town. A few bars were tucked in here and there, but the street was, for the most part, empty. We walked hand-in-hand in the rain, dodging the occasional awning edge that sent a wave of water onto those

---

* Don't drink and paddle.

directly below. Just two blocks before reaching the car, we found a shop that was still open. We had not noticed this antique store earlier in the day, and they showed no signs of locking up, so we ventured in.

Like most good antique stores, a musty scent pervaded the crowded maze of furniture, knick-knacks, books, clothing, and other junque. Unlike most antique stores, it was manned by a few unintentionally funny young guys, who seemed more likely to ask you to act in their independent film than to sell you a vintage crystal dish. We entered amid a joint effort to open a bottle of wine. They sounded like they had already started to sample some. "We just found this wine and we're trying to figure out if it's still any good," Guy #1 explained, though we had not asked. "You guys looking for anything in particular?" We shook our heads 'no' and continued to browse. A moment later we heard Guy #2 declare the most recent bottle "Good- for vinegar." They all laughed and opened another.

Maybe they would be open all night, or at least until the vino ran out. We were leafing through some books when I heard my favorite part of the conversation. It apparently had to do with the third guy's questionable status as a clergy member of one of the lesser known religions. "So did you ever get to marry anyone?" asked Guy #1.

"No, they broke up a week before the wedding," Guy #3 lamented, then quickly added, "but I'm still qualified!" With that, we sorted through a few more records, and bid our hosts good evening. It was time to head back for a long soak, and an even longer sleep.

Saturday morning the house was full. We again joined a dining room full of fellow breakfasters who didn't quite know what to make of us until they realized that we 1.)were productive members of society, 2.)had a deep respect for veterans, and 3.)were not going to hold band practice in the formal parlour. Number 2 was particularly meaningful. One gentleman at our table was in town for a reunion with his fellow Vietnam veterans. He was proud and had enjoyed a wonderful evening of catching up with his buddies the night before.

We were attentive listeners, but it was awkward when his wife tried to draw more information out of him than he cared to discuss. We tried to graciously transition because she-- though married to him for several decades-- couldn't take a hint from his quickly watering eyes and edgy movements. "He just never really talks about it," she explained to us as she patted his hand. *So what makes you think he wants to share the details of serving in hell with complete strangers?* Rule Number One when talking to veterans: say thanks and then shut up and listen. If silence is the only thing that's shared, then that's all you need to hear.

The conversation rounded itself out with other topics, thanks to the patrons' interest in each others' agendas for the day. We finished our coffee and went back to our room to mindlessly spend our final hour until checkout. It may or may not have involved a Steve Martin comedy, some smooching, and brief snoring. Soon, it was time to leave.

The only other event planned for the weekend was still an hour and a half off. Because we obviously did not learn our lesson two days prior, we hiked downtown in search of a good café in which to relax. We actually did find a place that we had previously bypassed, so we stepped inside, dodging the ever-growing crowds outside. I had consumed more than my share of coffee already that morning, but we needed to lend some legitimacy to our loitering, so in went the orders for two small black coffees.

I glanced around the room as I waited for our drinks. It was a sort of mercantile-shop-turned-art studio/café. Not bad, lots of white, but tasteful. Also lots of boobies-- in the paintings, I mean. While thousands of years of human visual arts have paid tribute to the natural female form, a little variation in the subject matter of the paintings would have been refreshing. We took our mugs to find a table, and I tried to position myself so as to forgo the view of any two-dimensional twins.

The grand finale of the weekend was to be a boat ride on the Mississippi River, departing from the dock at Chestnut Mountain Resort. I thought I would surprise Senator with a relaxing pontoon float, but there was some question as to whether or not the ride would be canceled. Fortunately, the flood waters which had buried the dock the week before had receded sufficiently since our arrival in Galena. I reserved our tickets over the phone, and we left town for the last time, via Jackass Road.

Chestnut Mountain is a strange place. On one hand, it is a viable and active resort, with a focus on the waterfront in the summer, and its steep ski hills in the winter.[*] On the other hand, it has a slightly creepy outdated and mysterious feel to it. For starters, their signage could have been a little more prominent. We missed the entrance twice, even with a map. The décor is also generically hey-look-we're-just-like-Colorado, and online reviews do not speak highly of the guest rooms. I suppose that is what happens when you build a ski resort in the lower Midwest.

As an added interest, however, there are options for transportation down to the waterfront. You can take a ski lift[†] or a long bobsled slide. While on the ski lift I learned, a little too late, that Senator is not at all comfortable hanging in a swinging cart with a single safety bar carelessly flipped over him, while dangling stories above the tree tops. Shoot. The topic had never come up. I can't say I blamed him. It was unnerving, especially when we noticed a few kids riding alone, safety bar still flipped

---

[*] Author vehemently denies existence of any certified mountains within the confines of the state of Illinois.

[†] which we accidentally took, due to a brief communication breakdown. Senator did not realize there were other options, and the flunkie who operated the lift failed to provide any useful guidance.

open.

The boat ride was far more serene. Twenty or so passengers rode gently on a pontoon boat as a local guide pointed out animals and plant life of interest. A strong eagle perched on one thick branch, eying us carefully. The guide also directed our attention to a vast patch of canary reed grass, a very invasive species that the Department of Natural Resources tried to eliminate via controlled burn, only to realize that it comes back even healthier and heartier when feeding on the nutrients of ashes. Oops.

The pontoon wove its way through back channels around islands. Due to their unique position and dense foliage, these islands are always about 10°F warmer than the mainland, and they maintain a 95% humidity reading. Yuck! That sounded especially oppressive during such an intensely steamy summer. The tour was ending, so the captain steered the boat around a bend and we glided our way back.

The most exciting part of the ride was just yards off the shore, though. Our able captain maneuvered the boat through the path he knew would prevent any hangups or damage. At least he intended to. Parked in the middle of the established route was a party boat, complete with arrogant partiers aboard. We were in for a standoff, but our captain wasn't about to back down. He quietly tried to squeeze past the stubborn boat as well as he could, but we did bump them slightly. There was no significant damage, but words you are not supposed to hear on a family-friendly pontoon outing were exchanged. I halfway expected them to attack like pirates, but that would have meant leaving their beer behind, so there was no threat.

We docked and thanked our guide for the tour. Another ski lift ride stood between us and the top of the mountain. The ride operator at the bottom was no more competent than our friend at the top. We secured our own bar and hoped for the best. The view was beautiful; we just would have appreciated it more under different circumstances. At the end of the line our bucket dumped us out safely, if awkwardly. Check ski lift off the list of adventures to experience together.

It was time to leave, and we were both ready to get home. I could not imagine the stress we would have encountered if we had taken the extended road trip we had originally planned. Our own mountain of unmixed recordings and unsorted lesson plans and student handouts awaited us at home. That was fine, though. There were still a few days at home together to work and play. We were still officially on vacation. In fact, we treated ourselves to a fantastic Mexican dinner just to prove it.

Chapter 6
No Kinda' Ground: Late February 2011

The fall semester sucked. There is no polite way of stating it. Being reluctantly hired back by a school board who worried about money when it came time to pay me, but had no problem spending more than I make in a year on a score board, was not good for my morale. I was also not looking forward to taking on the job of classroom aide in addition to my own. Cuts, cuts, you know. Not that that kept the administration from enrolling extra students in my class. Make do, make do, you know. By September I was swimming. Every day was a nonstop three-ring circus with myself as the only performer.

One night I announced to Senator that I believed the experience was either supposed to 1.)make me stronger/better, or 2.)prepare me for gladly accepting a lay-off if/when it came. A month later I declared that I was hoping it was the second one. In late October, when our program coordinator and my only friend at work left for ten weeks' maternity leave, adding to my work load, I went home and instituted a family meeting.

"Can you get three days off in February?" I asked Senator, scoping out the school year calendar magnet on the fridge.

"Yeah, that should be fine. Just write the dates down so I can request them off." *Everyone should have such a congenial travel companion.*

After hours of searching for the best value based on destination, time frame, and method of travel, I decided we were going to New York over Presidents' Day weekend. In planning the details, I realized that we had not been to New York in two and a half years. That, in itself, was outrageous. We had seen Spencer and Michelle several times since then, when they popped into Chicago for business or family events, but we needed to go *there*. I missed the city terribly. I wanted to walk down Broadway, holding Senator's hand, weaving expertly through the crowds of determined natives and lost tourists, while smelling the enticing aroma of roasted, sugared mixed nuts from street vendors.

CONFIRM. With a final and unnecessarily firm click of the mouse I solidified our reservations and my sanity. The holidays would be wonderful, January would initiate a new, better, more organized semester, and right around the corner, like your favorite deli, New York would be waiting.

As the big weekend approached, we were pleased and surprised to find that no home issues, natural disasters, or other catastrophes had occurred. *Well this is a nice change of pace.* Perhaps fate was giving us a break since we had worked so hard over the past several months. We were even packed early enough to enjoy an episode of *A Year in Provence*[*] (June, to be

---

[*] For the past two years it has been our tradition to watch the BBC miniseries *A Year in Provence* around Valentine's Day. Told in twelve months is the story of Peter and Annie Mayle, who chuck their grown-up London careers to start their dream life in southern France. Learning the language is nothing compared with learning the culture. After all, not every foreigner is easily accepted into the

precise), before going to bed early.

When the alarm clock went off at 3:00am, we were tired, but excited. In just hours we would be back in Manhattan, comfortably blending in among throngs of languages, colors, and backdrops. I couldn't believe we had been running around on these trips together for over seven years. Then again, I couldn't believe we had not been running around on these trips together our entire lives. *Maybe we could shave just a few more years off of our jobs before retirement.* Senator interrupted my thoughts. "Ready?"

"Always!" I grabbed my purse and he grabbed our suitcase. It seemed strange to be walking out the door together without an entourage of microphones, cables, and computer gear. We could get spoiled.

As is my habit when leaving the house for a trip, I mentally aligned the lists of what we would need vs. what I had packed. A three day jaunt with no real plans is easy to pack for though, so everything was in order. I pictured us at the airport, and double-checked to make sure our licenses were safely tucked away. Then I imagined going through security and... what?... setting off the metal detector?!

I never wear a belt, and I had no chains on me, but I did neglect the possibility that my British Union Jack shirt, outlined in sparkling red, white, and blue sequins might contain metal. This was a dilemma. It's not like I could take it off, and I was not about to pass through the human microwave body scanner. The time for action was then and there.

I explained my problem and proposed the solution to Senator, as he pulled the car into a space in the airport's overnight lot. "...So, I'm going to run back to the trunk, grab a

---

underground truffle scene. If you have ever taken a step of faith to achieve something you want with someone you love, you must watch this.

shirt from the suitcase, change in the car, and put the bling shirt back in the suitcase." He vaguely muttered in agreement, or defeat. "I just need you to watch for any approaching shuttle buses," I explained, indicating the drop-off station, which was roughly twenty paces from our car. Not that it mattered; I was probably on security cameras anyway.

I finagled one arm out of my shirt while keeping an eye on a distant bus. The right arm was slightly more challenging, as anyone who has ever changed clothes in a car[*] will tell you. Resembling Venus in my lack of arms only, I now braced for the big shift. The new shirt was poised on the ends of my arms. The metal shirt was creeping up for the cast-off. Success! Well, sort of. In the ballet of the moment, I somehow managed to give myself a painful pinch in my neck. Ouch! I rolled my head around from side to side like a low budget masseuse while we waited, correctly shirted, for the next shuttle.

The wind was blowing hard that Saturday. Fortunately, it did not make the ride too turbulent. While I have never been afraid to fly, I can do without the sudden drops and bumps. Overall, it was a smooth flight, though. In fact, the strong tail wind saved us about twenty minutes of flight time.

I did learn, however, that it is not a good idea for me to fly with an empty stomach. A small snack probably would have helped me during the ascent. As we climbed thousands of feet into the air, my ears popped often and I was forced to yawn repeatedly in order to catch my breath. Just about the time my breathing was under control, I started to get dizzy and the edges of my vision went dark. I quickly shook myself alert so I wouldn't pass out. I did not want Senator to worry, and I certainly did not want to make a scene on the plane. Knowing my luck, I would have ended up on the news. In retrospect, though, maybe I should have just gone with it, since I am never

---

* and yes, I realize that I've probably done this more than most.

able to sleep on planes.

By the time we claimed our bags, our friend Spencer was waiting outside to pick us up. It was great to see him, but we noticed the glaring absence of Michelle. As it turned out, we had come during New York's Fall Fashion Week. Anyone involved in the fashion industry was absorbed with buyers, sellers, out-of-town representatives, labels, and retailers all doing fashion-forwardy things. We would have to meet Michelle later that night.

In the meantime, we were hungry. The three of us drove to Brooklyn to a café near our friends' home. The cold wind was getting intense, making the thought of omelets and coffee all the more alluring. We slid into a corner booth in the crowded room.

After we ordered I excused myself to the restroom. The tiny bathroom was clean, and even homey, with a scented candle burning on the counter. As one who detests public bathrooms, I appreciated the extra touches. I then squirted a dab of soap on my hands and began to lather. Whoa! My hands immediately turned red and started to burn. I grabbed the bottle of soap, convinced I must have done something dumb like used toilet bowl cleaner. Nope. It was just hardcore peppermint soap. Drying my irritated hands, I wondered if anyone needed to be *that* clean.

After our meal, we went to Spencer's place to hang out. The seventh floor condo's many windows provided an excellent view of the snow, which was now blowing mercilessly sideways. Outside flower pots and chairs and various doggie toys blew around the deck. We helped corral what we could, bundling items together so they wouldn't become flying missiles over Brooklyn. Maybe, just maybe, I was ready for spring.

Inside we talked and visited. I enjoyed our conversation, which rambled from real estate, to politics, to music, to our distinct lack of fashion knowledge (here's to jeans and your favorite tee shirt), to a lot of other odds and ends. In the gaps, however, I was fading. I had forbidden myself to doze in the car or the airport terminal in hopes that I would sleep on the plane. No such luck, though. Now, it was hitting me hard. I required a good, solid nap. I glanced at Senator to assess his state. He concurred.

Though our friends are excellent and easygoing hosts, we opted to stay in a hotel for this trip. We wanted to spend time in Lower Manhattan, and we needed some time alone. Occasionally our lives get so busy that it seems we have to go on vacation just to see each other without projects looming over our heads. Mind you, the projects are self-inflicted things we enjoy, but they eat up time quickly, and it is a liberating experience to temporarily run away from one's home, studio, and computer.

We had several hours to sleep before meeting our friends again, and we took advantage of each one of them. I enjoyed a nap so deep that I was lost and confused when I woke up. Recognizing that I was at an inn in New York with Senator was a wonderful surprise. Now I was ready to go. "Where's the Weather Channel on this thing?" I asked, grabbing the remote control. I was ready to dance.

Soon Spencer picked us up. His friend Michael was with him. The next object was to collect Michelle. She was currently being held captive in a show in Chelsea, but we were about to spring her.

Spencer pulled up to the building and Michael, Senator, and I got out to go inside. The wind whipped through the side streets harder than before, and I struggled to close the car door. In the lobby, six stern and bitter looking men of various ages stared at us in unison. We nosed around a bit with no success, and they certainly were not offering any assistance. Finally Michael asked if they knew where the show was being held. "13th and 14th floor," one of them answered curtly and reluctantly. *Good thing there are six of you here to help people.*

We had a fifty-fifty shot, so we went to the 14th floor.

Sculpted girls with bad but no doubt expensive haircuts greeted*
us and told us it was on the 13th floor. Down we went, arriving
at a maze of very white rooms with booths of clothes, manned by
various representatives, most of whom were tall, thin, and blond.
Every time we thought we spied our friend around a corner, the
woman would turn to reveal a stranger. The place was crawling
with fake Michelles. Eventually we found the correct Michelle
and brought her down to the car. Just as we closed the last car
door, a large chunk of building material fell to the ground across
the street. It was time to vacate the scene.

    Everyone was hungry, and as long as the food was hot
and had never led a life of its own, I was in. Michael suggested
Korean food, and Spencer and Michelle were enthusiastic.
Senator and I were looking forward to trying a new cuisine, and
so we assumed the position of students. Gazing over the menu,
our best options seemed to be the curry veggie soup and some
noodle-veggie-egg concoction.

    What will stick out most in my mind when I henceforth
think of Korean food will be the ridiculous number of dishes on
the table. To begin with, our party of five was each served water,
green tea, and personal bowls of rice, establishing the dish count
at fifteen before any food had even been ordered. For each
normal (nonvegetarian) guest, the server brought a whole fish,
sort of the Korean answer to chips n' salsa while you wait.
Several different sauces were then placed on the table.

    Then the real fun began. We ordered sample appetizers,
which, apparently, each required their own small dish. Before
we were through with the appetizers, the entrees started to
arrive. No exaggeration, at least thirty dishes meshed together,
completely burying our once sizable table.

    Overcrowding aside, the food was refreshingly
unexpected. I know, I know. That sounds like I ripped it out of

---

* (term used loosely)

a cheap review guide, but it is an honest description. For example, I thought I knew everything there was to know about the preparation of broccoli, but I had never had it cold with a garlic marinade. I could have feasted on piles of that alone and been satisfied. I have also tasted various curries, but this curry veggie soup was a milder, smoother version than you would find in a typical Indian dish. While it was not as spicy as I would have liked, it was satisfying in a warm, comfort food sort of way.

We also tried kimchi, a staple dish that white people who try Korean food are excited to introduce to their other white friends. I mention this food for two reasons: 1.)Kimchi is yummy. 2.)It's the only dish whose name I remember. Kimchi is a slightly sweet, mostly sour, very delectable version of cabbage. In all honesty, it rivals a good Chicago Polish kraut. While we did not eat the seafood or beef, we are told that Korean cuisine knows how to pull off a mean barbecue, too. Watch out Texas.

When we had sufficiently dirtied enough plates to keep a full staff of dishwashers employed, we left the restaurant in search of the next adventure. As I have stated, Senator and I purposely neglected to make any solid plans, preferring to go with the flow on this trip. This may or may not have been wise. Nevertheless, we were on our way to see a band called the Bull Mastiffs at a place called Funkadelic Studios.

In between fighting with my chopsticks* and delighting in my tofu, I gleaned that we were going to see some live music. Good, good. I picked up that it was a friend of a friend's band or

---

* Believe it or not, I used to know how to successfully use chopsticks to eat. I'm not saying I could maneuver rice with them, but I was solidly competent. At the Korean restaurant, however, I became the equivalent of two year old Asian child who had suffered a stroke. Spencer's attempt to show me how to correctly hold the utensils only made things worse. While culinary history has not been kind to the spork, I would have gladly traded my sticks for the helpful plastic tool.

his roommate's band, or maybe even his dog's band, given the name. My expectations were not lofty; I was just looking for decent music and maybe a fun show. What completely escaped me between bites of vegetable tempura was that we were going to a studio, where the band would sort of rehearse and sort of put on a show for the public. Different.

Spencer parked the car and the five of us entered what looked like an empty building. Near the front there was an elevator, and one of the other four correctly surmised to which floor we were supposed to climb. The rickety cab carried us upward as the floors sped by in front of us, viewable through the round porthole windows. The elevator stopped and the door opened, revealing a small crowd milling around, and a girl at a table collecting cover fees.

"Is this the place?" asked one of us.

"This *smells* like the place!" answered Michael, simultaneously announcing our presence to the previously uninterested group. The air was perfumed partly with old NYC warehouse (good), pot (not so good), and musty musician sweat (definitely not good).

Funkadelic Studios contained a dozen or so small, insulated recording rooms. On this particular night, various bands and a few poets were practicing in the rooms. The rest of us were free to wander four hallways that formed a square, dropping in on performers when we felt the urge. In a sense, we served as a rotating audience.

Senator and I were trying to get a feel for the situation when a three person parade of outlandishly dressed band members in bad stage makeup came around the corner chanting their name and beating a drum. "Man-bur-ger. Sur-gi-cal." *(thump-thump-thump)*. Senator and I looked at each other. No words were necessary here. It was kind of like being at a college party with people who thought they were making a talented statement.

When the Manburgers had passed, we squeezed our way into a room that featured jazz. My first impression was that it was a few guys having fun, but nothing very interesting. I guess the past two years of trailing Senator as he records great international jazz artists has spoiled me. Unintentionally, I am becoming quite the improv critic.

Just then someone asked if anyone played drums. Spencer, Michelle, and I zoned in on Senator. It wasn't Liberace's piano,[*] but it could be a fun moment. In the room, a woman with a clipboard seemed to be making notes and trying to keep things organized. Senator looked at me. "Should I?" he shrugged.

"Why not?" was my fast response. By the time he overcame his humility and agreed to play, Michelle was handing him a set of drumsticks, borrowed or purloined from another room. Senator went to let Clipboard Lady know he would play.

Here is where the experience, which had not to this point, been particularly superb anyway, took a dive. Clipboard Lady promptly informed Senator of the 'rules', and that certain time slots were accounted for, and even though this was a random group of trumpet blowers and upright bass bangers, he might have to wait until she was ready. "Okay, never mind." So much for the free spirit of improvisational music. So much for helping out a struggling group. Maybe it is better that he did not play. He would have shown them up too badly anyway.

For lack of other options, we made the rounds a few more times, poking our heads into the occasional studio. One room had two drummers going, and I was interested, but the sound was so muddy that I had to go back out into the hall to hear it. As I stood alone in the hallway, cigarette smoke leaked through from the illegally designated smoking room. A guy wandered by and invited me into the poetry room. I smiled and politely declined, deciding that my next room would be the elevator.

---

[*]   See *How to Change a Flat on a Unicycle*

My eyes burned. Soon Senator and the others emerged from the drum room. Senator looked at me and read my thoughts, but for the sake of humor asked, "What d'ya think, V?" He grinned, and then laughed at my anticipated answer.

"This pretty much sucks, Z." I laughed and told him I would patiently wait downstairs for them. No one had to hurry on my account, but I was done with Funkadelic Studios. As it turned out, so were Spencer, Michelle, and Senator. They followed me back to the front of the square, and back to the elevator. We never did see Bull Mastiffs. I guess they were following Manburger Surgical at a later time slot. Clipboard Lady probably knew.

As we climbed into the back seat of Spencer and Michelle's car, I was grateful to be getting back to the hotel. Wind and smoke had burned my eyes to a lovely heroin-addict red. I snuggled up close to Senator in the back seat. It was hard to tell whose hair was in worse shape. The next morning would be our time. As for the rest of the night, the History Channel documentary on Hitler's bodyguards wasn't just going to watch itself. We cuddled on the bed as the Third Reich began its fall.

Sunday morning I was in and out of the shower, dressed, and ready before I had even intended to be awake. Senator had not noticed that I was out of bed. I was glad he was sleeping. Once we got home he would be working ten days in a row, followed by a five day recording tour.

After a while, Senator got up and got ready. We were on our own until the afternoon, so the plan was to find food and then visit Trinity Church. We made a quick coffee stop at the hotel's breakfast bar, but the cold cereal and stale muffins did not sound as appealing as finding a deli or café in the neighborhood. We bundled up and stepped outside. Thankfully, the winds had died down for the most part.

The ironic thing about the Financial District is that weekends are the quietest time to visit. During the week Wall

Street is king, ruling the economic communities of the world as business travelers scurry about. Restaurants thrive and hotels are booked full. On a Sunday morning in February, however, you can own the streets, provided you do not expect much to be open.

We walked for several blocks before finding a café that specialized in fresh, organic ingredients. As we enjoyed our cheesy[*] breakfast sandwiches and more coffee, we plotted our day. After much unnecessary figuring, we decided that we could make it to a service at Trinity on time, and then hang around doing some more nothing. I finished my coffee and stuffed a few stiff napkins into my purse for the inevitable runny noses that the cold air always brings out in us.

It was a short walk to Trinity Church, but the shadows of the buildings kept a cold sting in the air. We ducked inside at the first opportunity. Service did not start for another hour, but we had nowhere else to be, so we slipped into a side pew. It reminded me of the lyrics to *California Dreamin'*: "...the preacher likes the cold; he knows I'm gonna' stay..." Even with the current February weather we were not longing for California, though. New York felt as right as L.A. felt wrong. Here, all we had to do was take in the sweet, smooth music of the choir.

A pipe organ played, too, but we were confused as to why the sound was coming from the front at the altar when the giant pipes were along the wall behind us. Could sound bounce that strangely? I slipped my jacket off, finally warming up. Once seated, it was fairly easy to hide the fact that we were wearing jeans. My glittery Union Jack shirt (take #2) was another story. I was striking out with this particular piece of apparel. What are the odds that I would don the flag of the one country who had raided the Lower Manhattan Dutch settlement, burning

---

[*] We had been on vacation over twenty-four hours and we had consumed no cheese. This needed to be remedied fast.

down the original Trinity Church?*

After a while the music restarted, signaling that the service had officially begun. It was nice to sit in a church where so many races and nationalities were represented. While New York maintains many ethnic communities, it never seems as segregated as Chicago. Surely God must approve of this arrangement.

A female pastor took the elaborately carved neo-Gothic pulpit. She began with a personal story about her childhood. She told us about a perfectionist drive toward getting good grades. "A 'B' was failing in my mind," she explained. I sat up to pay attention. Senator shot a glance at me and smirked. He knew this was a woman who understood me.

She went on to talk about the difference between a hopeless, self-centered perfectionism, and a true, selfless quest for excellence. I thought about everything Senator and I had taken on in the past year. The recording gigs were coming more frequently, but we seemed to be managing our time well. School was still very consuming, but I had been able to step back some of the workload. I took a deep breath. It was good to be reminded of the gift of balance and the privilege to fail occasionally.

It was a long, ceremonious Episcopalian service. The procession of clergy, altar attendants, and others, set against such magnificent architecture was an awe-inspiring sight. I drank in the experience. The previous night we were in a crappy, stinky warehouse studio. Now, we sat in one of the most beautiful, historically significant houses of worship in the country. God bless America!

At some point in the service, a leader announced that a docent would be available afterward to give a tour to anyone

---

* Pretty good if you are Wendy V, and no, we would not have dressed so bummy if we had planned on attending church.

who was interested. O happy day, indeed! Senator wanted to do this as well, so we penciled it into our empty agenda. I looked down, and subtly buttoned my jacket over the blazing British bars.

When everyone had filed out of the pews, we stepped out of our row. Actually, Senator stepped out of our row. Whether by sheer clumsiness, my giddiness at the prospect of touring my favorite church, or being tripped by a patriot ghost who spied my Tory shirt, I missed the step and plunged out into the aisle. Senator turned quickly to catch me, managing to break my fall into four sort of slow motion lapses.

It was so fast and unexpected. My leg hurt, and I coughed from the violent motion. A kind older couple asked if I was okay. I could nonchalantly tell that I would be alright, but for the moment I was a kid who had fallen off her bike, nodding while blinking back tears. Adding insult to injury was the glaring irony of tripping in full view of the graceful stained glass angels and saints. *Poor child. She obviously wasn't born on a Tuesday...*[*]

I recovered quickly and we met Katie for our tour. Closer to the front of the sanctuary, we could see that the floor was inlaid parquet wood. The back wall of the altar could rival that in any European cathedral. Stained glass illustrated Bible scenes, and stone and wood carvings all around held hidden meanings. A person could spend hours dissecting the altar images alone.

We moved on to the pipe organ. Our question about the sound was about to be answered. From 1848, when this particular building was constructed, until September 11, 2001, the original pipes in the back of the room boomed out the notes of the organ. Then the Twin Towers were heinously attacked, leaving too much residue inside the pipes for them to properly

---

[*] See traditional children's poem *Monday's Child*, attributed to the enigma Mother Goose

function. Rather than spend the $2,000,000 to have them restored, the church spent a tenth of that for a digital translator for the organ, and used the rest to help the devastated community.

The tour moved through the rest of the premises, past an elaborate chapel reserved for silent reflection and meditation. In another room, headstones that had been rescued from the elements of the adjacent graveyard hung on the walls. Among them was Alexander Hamilton's stone. We then walked back through the sanctuary. I craned my neck and looked everywhere at once, the way most tourists do when they are walking *outside* on the streets of New York. Finally we reached the last portion of our tour, which centered on the formidable doors at the back and sides of the church. Each depicted a scene from the city's and/or the church's early days. Taking a few moments to concentrate on the intricate details left us amazed.

It was time to journey outside again. The air had not warmed up, but the sun was streaming down onto the street as we left Trinity. We hesitated for a minute, satisfied that we had enjoyed such a peaceful morning together among a sea of strangers. Then, at the same second, Senator and I smiled enthusiastically in recognition of our favorite New York treat.

On the corner of Broadway and Wall was a Nuts4Nuts! vendor. As in past visits, we were hooked the moment we smelled the roasted, sweet-coated mixed nuts. In the time we had been away from New York, Nuts4Nuts! had ramped it up by including chunks of coconut. Just steps away from the church, avarice took over.

There is no way I'm sharing a bag. I want my own! Before I could voice my greedy intentions, Senator beat me to it. "And none of this sharing crap. We're each getting our own bag!" Who was I to argue? I slung my purse over my shoulder to effectively dig out each warm morsel from the palm-sized bag. Manna.

We had a few hours free until our next adventure, which was good because it required some strategic planning. The assignment was to meet our friends uptown later that afternoon, so I went to work plotting our subway route. Within a block or two of our hotel we could catch a train that would stop just a block from our destination. It had been a while since we navigated the underground, so we left early to be on the safe side.

The great thing about the New York subway system is that it is so expansive, making the boroughs very accessible.* The not-so-great thing about any public transportation, however, is that you are at the mercy of changes, interruptions in schedule, and construction. On this particular day, construction in Midtown had shut down part of our line. We could still get where we needed to go, but there were about three times as many people as there should have been trying to squeeze onto each train.

I shrugged. It was all part of the experience. What could we do? At least it was warmer than the street. Make that much warmer. We crammed inside and I held on to Senator, who in turn held on to a small free space on the pole in the rear of the car. I braced my feet to prevent falling into someone when the train braked, but I suppose that was not necessary since there was not any room to fall. Since the train had to make all of the local stops, we were in for a good half hour of cheap entertainment.

Chief in my memory of our fellow riders was Angry Girl. This girl was about eighteen years old, of Bronx persuasion, and convinced that it was her duty to spew venomous retorts at anyone who dared to enter her three inch bubble of space. Overcrowding conditions what they were, this basically included

---

* The NYC subway system contains over 650 miles of regularly used rail.

everyone. "Wha do you think yaw doin'?!" Angry Girl screamed at a kindly gentleman, who seemed confused. She then delivered a diatribe about "all of these people who better just stay themselves back."

Some of Angry Girl's rhetoric came from a quasi-protective thing she had going on as well. Angry Girl, it seemed, was friends with Baby Mama. Baby Mama, in her infinite teenage wisdom, had carted her baby, stroller and all, onto the train, taking up valuable floor space, and subjecting the child to stagnant, stuffy air. Angry Girl was appalled that people were standing next to the baby-- as if they had a choice-- so she screamed about that some more.

Then there were the stops every few minutes. The automatic doors would slide open, we would hear the passengers on the platform utter an audible groan in unison, and the doors would close again. No one got off, so no one could get on. We all understood the physics of the situation, but that did not stop Angry Girl from yelling to those outside the car. "No one is getting' in hee-yah! Tha' ain't no room! Damn stoopit peoples!"

Baby Mama stayed quiet, which only perturbed Angry Girl further. "Why ain't you care about these f*@#in' people goin' up by yer baby? Damn, if that was my baby,[*] I would be snappin' and goin' off on these people!" *You don't say.*

Not all of the conversations we overheard were so filled with angst. There was also Birthday Girl and her friend. Birthday Girl casually asked her friend if she would go with her on a cruise for her birthday. While not unpleasant, her friend shut down that idea in no uncertain terms.

"Giiiirrrrl! Hell no I ain't goin' on no cruise! There is no kinda' ground under there- just water! I can't even swim!" She then offered alternatives. "I mean, I'll come to a *basement* party,

---

[*] (Heaven help the poor spawn)

or a *club* party, but I ain't goin' on no boat."

Before Birthday Girl could respond, her friend thought of further support for her argument. "Giiiirrrrl! Ain't you never seen *Titanic*? There is a lesson there. All those people drownded and that is a real story!"

Finally, just in case there was any doubt as to her position on the issue, she added one last point definitively. "Black people don't go on cruises!" *Hhmmm.* I had never thought about it as a race issue before. Such was our lesson in subway culture under less-than-ideal conditions.

When we reached our stop, we carefully untangled ourselves from the web of passengers. We had to move quickly to get out of the car before the doors closed again, trapping us with more writing material. It was a short walk to the Park Avenue Armory, where we were going to see some sort of musical performance that I knew little about. As long as it didn't involve chanting painted men in smoky studios, I was willing to give it a shot.

The Park Avenue Armory is worth going to see just for the merits of the building. Built at the beginning of the Civil War as a military facility and gentlemen's social club, it houses grand reception rooms straight out of a Victorian novel. Inside are beautiful art works of silver and other metals, along with fireplaces to rival those of Citizen Kane. The centerpiece of the armory is a 55,000 square foot drill hall, which boasts the claim of being one of the largest unobstructed spaces in the city.

On this afternoon, the hall was transformed into an interactive acoustic concert. We were expecting a few dozen attendees, but we watched hundreds of patrons flood into the drill hall in anticipation of a unique musical experience. Throughout the room drums and cymbals were stationed. There did not appear to be an exact front, so people started to gather in a circle around the center of the floor. Some chose to sit down, and others stood. Spencer, Michelle, Senator and I were on the sit-stand border, but we were content to stand.

Just as it seemed that something was about to start, a persnickety older lady tapped Michelle, informing her flatly that, "people are sitting down." Well, we weren't. Deal with it. After the Funkadelic Studios adventure, I was keeping my escape routes open.

Soon several people who were scattered among the crowd started making soft swooshing sounds. This evolved into swinging plastic pipes to make a sort of haunting chorus. It was kind of like hearing the neighborhood kids playing, only in a pleasant, melodic tone. This could be interesting.

The next phase increased the dynamics somewhat. Nearby a college-aged hipster began swirling an upside down snare drum filled with garbanzo beans. Again, not an unpleasant aural sensation. Having been introduced to the finer points of creative sound by Senator and his passion for free jazz, I was willing to listen to that for awhile.

What I was not willing to do was make interactive eye contact with him while he edged closer and closer to me, vying for a reaction. I caught Michelle's giggle out of the corner of my eye. She knew me. *Okay, Bean Boy, I like your sound, and I can even dig your performance art, but I have just enough New York in me to tell you where to stuff those chickpeas if you intrude my personal bubble.* I won. Bean Boy moved on in deference to my steely observation.

Gradually the music swelled into a full orchestral sound, filling the hall with amorphous tones which blended beautifully. There were performers on the main floor of the drill hall and along the balcony. More spilled out through the reception rooms and galleries. The best part was that the audience now understood that they could wander around freely among the ultimate surround sound concert.

Senator and I took advantage of this condition to explore the rest of the building. Overall, I was surprised and intrigued.

Staged in a different manner, this could have been an obnoxiously pretentious event. Instead, the group hosted a comfortable scene in which they could share their creations with an appreciative and receptive audience.

After the concert, the night was yet young, but the four of us weren't so sure we were. For various reasons all of our schedules had been hectic recently. A late night out did not sound appealing, especially since Michelle had to get up early to greet the fashionistas. Thus, it was unanimously decided that we would grab some pizza, and then head back to our friends' home for coffee.

Of course, we were still on vacation. Even a quiet evening with friends demanded something sweet. An emergency run to the local bakery yielded butterscotch and dark chocolate-dipped cookies. I dunked my dessert. Not unlike my initiation into the wonders of fondue, I quickly learned that my ability to balance drenched morsels of food leaves something to be desired. PLOP! I shrugged and drank my coffee to get to the butterscotch mush at the bottom.

We were all relaxed, including their dog. In fact, the only sudden move he made was to guard his chew bone when I walked past it. Once assured that I was not after his treat, he slumped back in his comfortable heap.

It was too cold to go out on the roof for a fire, but the Manhattan skyline sparkled just the same. It had been a fast weekend. When we compared schedules with our friends, it did not look like we would be able to get together the next day, which would be our last day in New York. Perhaps the spring would bring more free time. March? April? Summer?

We said our goodbyes and crawled into the back of the car we had called to take us back to our hotel. It had been a good music day. It had been a good day. I leaned against Senator and watched the colors of the buildings go past. Suddenly I had the urge to take a walk with him. The February air curtailed the urge somewhat, but not completely. "You can let us out right here," I told the driver. I pulled my hat down over my ears as we fast-walked the last two blocks to the hotel.

Monday morning we turned on the news while we got ready. The local broadcast showed snowy scenes from all over the city. I grabbed the curtain and swept it back. Overnight it had snowed about two inches-- two very wet, heavy inches that coated the trees with a thick, bright layer. On the news people were sharing their woes at more snow, but I was reveling in the chance to see a wintry New York. We had already experienced it in spring, summer, and autumn. Now the cycle was complete.

We left the inn and walked the easy block to the subway station. We needed to head to the edge of Chinatown to a jazz music store called Downtown Music Gallery. Had it been warmer, we would have planned to walk the entire way, but the dampness suggested we take a train. Once again, however, we were at the mercy of construction rerouting.

The first station was closed for construction. This made things a bit tricky as not very many routes led to our desired neighborhood. We turned down a side street. Two more stations were closed. It was early yet, and the store did not open until noon, so we decided to walk along Broadway until we found a place to grab a bite to eat. That would kill time and move us closer to an available subway stop.

Half an hour and many blocks later we still had not found anything suitable in the way of food. At least we were making progress in the general direction of our destination, but now we were in Chinatown. This, in itself, was not a bad thing, but if you are a vegetarian looking for a 'safe' meal, plucked ducks hanging in storefront windows do not inspire confidence.

My fingers were getting cold and my tissue supply was reduced to thin, pathetically damp strands surrounding large holes. "Can we pop into Starbucks for a minute?" I asked. Senator agreed. I needed to regroup.

I rubbed my fingers for warmth, stole a few fresh napkins, and consulted the map. At this point it looked like we were committed to walking the entire distance to Downtown Music Gallery. We now stood at the intersection where we would have had to get off the train and walk the rest of the way anyway. The store's location was actually not convenient to anything save the East River, if you happen to be swimming by... which no living body ever would be.

We warmed up a little longer and then stepped back outside. A block or two later I had a happy revelation. The smell of garlic suddenly dominated the air. I had forgotten that Chinatown bordered Little Italy. If we just turned up a side street, the scene would change drastically, and we might even find a tempting spot for lunch.

We turned north and wandered along the row of ristorantes and cafés. Casually we browsed the menus posted in the windows. "Will you like to have lunch today?" A friendly, accented voice broke into our thoughts.

"Possibly..." The owner of a small café began to rattle off specials while opening his arms to usher us into his establishment. "Actually, we're vegetarians," began Senator. This seemed to delight the man even more. He highlighted his meatless options with grand enthusiasm, braving the elements to secure customers.

Senator and I looked at each other and smile-shrugged. Why not? There were probably a dozen great places to eat on the block, and they probably all served the same basic dishes. We might as well give our business to the owner making the greatest effort.

The act continued inside the restaurant. "Oh I have a lovely table for you by the windows!" We glanced around. An available window seat was not a particularly miraculous sight in the almost-empty dining room of about eight tables, half of which were by the windows. Still, it was warm and cozy, and it smelled wonderful. The scene was made complete when the Godfather peeked out from the kitchen. The senior and very Italian member of the organization took a brief, silent survey of the room and then retreated. We must have passed his inspection.

Senator and I dove into our cheese ravioli and capellini with broccoli and pesto. We had not eaten since the light dinner the night before, and our noses and our stomachs prompted us to keep going. It was delicious. I just needed one more small hunk of bread to dunk in my olive oil, pepper, and parmesan. Divine. Dessert would have been too much, but we ordered espresso to round it all out.

As we sat sipping our caffe, we looked out the window. There, in the middle of the street, the post-meal entertainment was unfolding before us. The restaurant owner from across the street was hollering in Italian at our owner. And yes, his arms were flying.* From the context clues, we gathered that he was upset that our owner was stealing business away from him by hitting up tourists in the street, as he had done with us. Perhaps if he was not enticing them into his restaurant, they might walk a few more feet to this guy's place. Our owner defended himself well, saying his piece and stubbornly returning to his post to court more hungry pedestrians.

It was getting heated. Now Other Owner brought in an ally. Ally had his own restaurant two doors down from our owner. He agreed with Other Owner, shaking his head vehemently to emphasize their solidarity against the perceived unfair labor practices.

No problem. Our guy just smiled and waved over at *his* ally, who happened to be on the opposite side of the street, not far from Other Owner. It was all getting very complicated, and

---

* As a partial Italian who would be mute if she ever lost her hands, I have every right to include this seemingly stereotypical detail.

we found ourselves in the middle of a square of feuding Italian provinces. *No wonder the empire fell.* The funniest part was that all of this squabbling among fellow countrymen took place under bright banners displaying the Roman monogram "S.P.Q.R.",[*] ironically recalling the glory of the former empire. ...And to think that I saw it on Mulberry Street.

We left the restaurant and reentered Chinatown. The music store was only another ten minutes away by foot. I navigated the diagonal streets back into the residential areas, and soon Senator and I were on Downtown Music Gallery's street-- not that you could tell. The only indication of the store was the address.

"I guess this is the place," Senator concluded. He had often ordered cds from the store, and wanted to browse the stock in person, but we had expected a slightly more prominent space. Steep steps led to a basement, with a buzzer on the locked door. We rang and were let in.

Inside, two short rows and the surrounding shelves and bins comprised the public section of the store. It was about the size of a moderate living room. One employee sat on a stool behind a counter. He wasn't going to win any hospitality awards, but he did offer assistance. We thanked him and browsed on our own. I wandered around quietly, aware of my stomach and wishing I had not eaten so much at lunch.

Fifteen or twenty minutes later, Senator thanked the employee and told me that he was ready to go. We had not counted on this. We both figured it would be a two hour excursion. "I think I preferred the mystery of the place, when all I knew of it was long distance orders." He did not buy a single piece of music. Then again, he probably already had most of it, or was about to record it.

---

[*] Senatus Populus que Romanus (translation: Daver is extremely well known among Romans.)

128

We climbed back out of the stairway and started walking to the main street back toward the hotel. We had not heard from our friends, so we decided to try for an earlier flight back home. There was nothing else we cared to do, and Senator now confessed that his stomach was bothering him quite a bit. *Hhmmm. This could be trouble.* We decided a cab was in order, but we agreed that we would continue walking until we spotted an available one. Maybe the fresh air would do us good, too. Yes, we were ready to go home.

After hiking for some time, we found ourselves in the Financial District. We never did get a cab. Between not finding an available train on the way up, and no cab on the way back, we had put in a few good miles on foot. Finally our inn was in sight. We retrieved our suitcase from the front desk, and in five minutes we were in a cab on the way to the airport.

"LaGuardia, please," I told the driver. Interestingly (and sometimes annoyingly), many taxis now have televisions in their back seats. Ours rambled on with a newscast that did not catch our attention until it mentioned delayed flights. Southwest had not posted any notices about our flight being delayed, but according to the reporter, nothing was moving in or out of Chicago quickly.

The story at the airport was worse. The ticket counter attendant informed us that, not only could we not get on an earlier flight, but our 6:15pm departure was not leaving until 11:00pm or so. "So there is nothing earlier we can take to Chicago?" I repeated back, to confirm that I had understood correctly.

"Well, I can get you on the 7:30pm, which is leaving at about 8:00pm."

Now I was really confused. "So, the flight that is scheduled *after* ours is now leaving *before* ours?" He nodded in confirmation as though this was the most natural logic in the world. "Alright, put us on the 7:30pm then." We did not understand, but we did not care, especially now that neither of us felt very well.

Security lines were not too long, but we had plenty of time to kill anyway. It was only about 3:00pm, so we staked our claims to two chairs. The terminals were filling up quickly with people delayed from traveling to numerous places. Planes were arriving late, and planes were departing even later.

In between reading and attempting to doze, we took advantage of the primary sport of air travelers-- people watching. A large woman in a Barney purple jogging suit swooped her way through the aisles of chairs with too much carry-on luggage. A good-natured little boy talked his big brother into sharing his headphones with him. He kicked his feet and bobbed his head merrily to the music, even after his brother pulled out the plug and walked away, leaving him with a mute earbud. For the most part, the crowd was agreeable for a group of inconvenienced passengers, but this was no consolation to Senator, who was getting sicker by the hour.

At last our plane was boarding. It was 8:30pm, which meant that we could still get a reasonable amount of sleep before work the next morning. Maybe we could even snooze during the flight. That, of course, would depend on the dozens of teenagers with whom we were sharing a flight. A high school band from New York, excited about their upcoming competition, filed into the plane with instruments and electronic gadgets in tow. Fortunately, a polite, quiet girl sat with us. While I love teenagers, I was too focused on Senator to appreciate their contribution to the arts.

He was in bad shape. I was mad at myself for allowing us to take his car to the airport. That meant he would have to drive the seventy miles back home, since I did not know how to drive a stick shift. I looked at him apologetically. He was pale and shivering now, even though he had both of our coats wrapped around him. I had never seen him so sick, and it was unnerving me. "How about we get a hotel by the airport tonight, and call off of work tomorrow? Then we won't have to drive home tonight."

Senator was weak, and his eyes were closed, but he still answered me emphatically. "No way! I'm sleeping in my own warm bed tonight." I guess we would have to play it by ear.

After what seemed like five hours, our 1 hour 45 minute flight landed. We got off the plane as quickly as possible. Senator now had renewed purpose as we fast-walked down to the baggage carousel. Moments later we were on the shuttle to the parking lot. He looked a little brighter. Anything was better than being on the plane.

The shuttle driver cautioned everyone about the roads. Chicago had experienced that wonderful 'wintry mix' that meteorologists cannot quite define. Pellets of ice fell from the sky and randomly turned to puddles or ice patches, depending on their moods. I almost slipped as we walked the short distance to our car.

"Are you absolutely sure you don't want to stay here and drive home tomorrow?" I offered one more time.

"No way!" came the consistent reply. We got into the car and turned on news radio. The biggest story was the weather, and the various spin-outs and accidents along I-55. Great. Senator had to drive cautiously, but that meant it would take even longer. I vowed that, from now on, we would only take my car anytime we traveled more than fifteen minutes from home.

Finally we were home. It was after 11:00pm, but we had made it safely. Everything was left sitting in the kitchen. I didn't bother to unpack anything but our driver's licenses and credit cards.

As tired as he was, Senator did not sleep well. I was glad the next morning when he told me he was calling off sick from work. I still did not feel great myself, and left work after half a day. On the way home, I stopped for ginger tea and apple juice, which turned out to be the only thing Senator could keep in his stomach.

As we sipped our tea, he told me that he had briefly talked to Michelle. She and Spencer had also been very sick. That explained why we had never heard from them Monday. From the sound of it, I was the one who had gotten off easiest. A solid three hour nap had essentially cured me. I looked at Senator and held his hand, which now felt a little bit stronger than before. "I guess this one wasn't our best trip, huh?" Still, we had enjoyed some great moments. Now we had to focus on recovery, as we had a different sort of trip coming up in nine days. This time, it would be a working vacation.

Chapter 7
Bonus!:
Early March 2011

Here we go. Once and only once I will provide, free of charge to my faithful reading public, a bonus chapter. Often I have mentioned that I tag along with Senator as a barely useful roadie during recording gigs. Early in 2011, he confirmed that he would record a jazz ensemble for five days in March. Performances would take place at various venues in Chicago and Milwaukee. Groups would range from duos to a ten piece combination.

Senator secured the time off of work without a problem. As for my job, it would be a little trickier to take time off from teaching. If I played my cards right, however, I would only have to miss one day of work, along with many hours of sleep. I could deal with that because I was not about to miss one of Senator's most significant recording sessions... or the chance to run away with him again for a few days.

The days leading up to the tour were packed with getting everything else done at home, making sure things were ahead of schedule at work, and preparing for myriad unforeseen technical problems that might arise. Finally, the first day arrived. Senator was home. Having worked out physically and mentally, he was ready. I worked that day, but I was just as eager to get going. So here, for your amusement, is a brief presentation of five days in the mobile recording world of One Room Studio.

Wed 4:15pm~ Senator greets me at the door with a kiss, and I'm so excited I can barely hold still while he hugs me. I have a very good feeling about all of this, and yes, I'm proud of the guy.

Wed 4:30pm~ Before I get too comfortable, I force myself to dive into my workout routine, determined not to miss my committed number of days per week. I shower, eat too fast, and we're off.

Wed 7:45pm~ We arrive at The Hideout in Chicago. Setting up is a bit tricky at first, as we have to work around the Soup Night people. Every Wednesday in winter, before the "late night jazz guys" play, various groups host an open soup and bread dinner. It smells delicious, but they are clearing out, and we are focused on our mission.

Wed 8:10pm~ As the band arrives, Senator asks the leader about set order, since the first three nights contain a vaguely named "Ad Hoc Unit". He gives us the rundown for the night, and then realizes he has not informed the other nine members that they will be recorded live... on everything they play for the next five days. Fortunately, all members are absolute gentlemen, and no musician egos interfere. In fact, they are downright appreciative.

Thurs 1:30am~ Attacked with a serious case of the munchies, we hold a brief, impromptu family meeting and unanimously vote for eating potato chips on the road home. Not a proud moment, but salty and satisfying nonetheless.

Thurs 2:45am~ We pull into the alley behind our house to unload the car. While we could probably leave the equipment in the middle of the yard for a week without anyone stealing it, the cold temperatures rule out leaving anything outside overnight. We make a few trips between the car and the basement. We're tired but ecstatic at how smoothly everything is going. Hopefully that will continue throughout the rest of the tour.

Thurs 3:00am~ The alarm clocks are both set, loudly, to wake me up on time for work. We should go to sleep, but...

Thurs 6:15am~ I slap the snooze button once, fully aware that an extra nine minutes will not an ounce of difference make. I stumble to the closet on autopilot, scooping up the clothes that I have already picked out to wear. Before leaving I inform Senator that he *must* take a nap today. We can't both be tired after tonight's performance.

Thurs 7:30pm~ We arrive a little early to Elastic in Chicago. Parking is easy, but load-in is a little rough here. There are about twenty steps that Senator has to navigate while carrying some pretty clunky gear. I sincerely pray he does not slip. I can't imagine...

Thurs 9:00pm~ We are arranged behind the scenes in our recording booth bunker, enjoying more great music. Now the fatigue sets in. The chair is a bit too comfortable, and I start to doze. One of the band members, who is waiting offstage for his set to begin, catches me fading and teases me. I might be embarrassed if other members weren't intermittently doing the same thing. Some of them have come from Europe, and the jet lag and rigorous schedule is taking its toll. Still, they all play superbly.

Fri 3:00am~ We are back home and unloaded. This time we check to make sure the alarms are *not* set, and then collapse into bed.

Fri 8:00am~ I am annoyed that I am up way too early. I blame in on the mixture of adrenaline and stupid dreams that forced me to escape them the only way one can escape a dream. 8:00am?! My body does not do this naturally.

Fri 12:00noon~ At least we have plenty of time to get ready. We add a clothes bag and some toiletries to the entourage of microphones, computer parts, cables, duct tape, and stands.

135

We are off to Milwaukee, making one quick pit stop for more backup hardware, just in case.

Fri 3:00pm~ We check into an Irish Inn, and thanks be to Jasus, Mary, Joseph, and all the blessed saints of Éire for the bonny green room-darkening shade on the window. The nap is instantaneous.

Fri 6:00pm~ We leave the inn for The Sugar Maple, just five miles away. As we are setting up in the small back room, we are curious as to how all ten members will fit on this tiny, non-raised stage together.

Fri 11:00pm~ The answer to our previous question: very carefully. I'm guessing those people in the front row got the full experience once the trombone spit started flying.

Sat 12:30am~ We have the luxury of setting up microphones in the back room and leaving them there in preparation for the next show, which will take place at the same venue. We have plenty of time to sleep in tomorrow morning (for a pleasant change), so we enjoy a drink (our only of the year) with a few of the European musicians. I love the outside perspective on the United States, and I hate that I have not been to Europe yet. Cheers, Mikolaj!

Sat 2:00am~ We are actually in bed relatively early for a recording night. Lying next to Senator, I realize how much I love doing this. I have always worked very well alongside of him, in both formal and informal settings. Assisting him with something he is so passionate about inspires me, and I have the added benefit of exploring new music that fascinates me. Too bad we have to keep working real jobs to support this (very) nonprofit habit. Senator keeps it all in perspective, though. As he puts it, "Any fool can work for money." Yes, we deserve each other.

Sat 9:00am~ Time for a leisurely breakfast and a long whirlpool soak. We are so impressed with the cleanliness, excellent food, hospitable staff, and conveniently arranged room at the inn, we book two more nights in anticipation of another recording weekend in June.*

Sat 1:00pm~ We arrive back at The Sugar Maple and set up in the spacious front room, employing sixteen channels and at least as many angels. We are maxed out for this project, but everything goes well and the Resonance Ensemble rocks the house. The energy is electric... or is that a burning cable?...

Sat 6:00pm~ We pack up again and return to the inn. This time we have to haul all of our gear up to our room, which is quite a trick when it comes to squeezing between cars in the overcrowded parking lot.

Sat 7:30pm~ Exhaustion sets in after dinner, but Senator still takes time to set up the computer in our room and back up the files. It would be awful to lose such great recorded material, not to mention highly unprofessional. The computer chugs along and I start to doze off as VH1 counts down the 100 Most Shocking Moments in Rock History.†

Sun 7:00am~ We are up early to get ready, grab a bite to eat, check out, and maneuver the gear back into our car.

Sun 9:00am~ We leave Milwaukee for the Chicago Cultural Center, amid nasty late winter wind.

Sun 11:00am~ We are on a high again, looking forward to the ensemble's performance in an auditorium. We start to unload gear through a maintenance entrance, and the security guard, who is about four times my size, insists that I give him my driver's license while we borrow an industrial cart. I'm pretty sure he could coax the cart back from me if I was suddenly taken with the nerve or inclination to steal it, but we comply.

Sun 1:00pm~ I wander the halls of the Chicago Cultural

---

* Don't worry, though. I'll only bore you with this one chapter on recording.

† Incidentally, I am appalled to learn that John Lennon's death (#2) was outranked by Michael Jackson's death (#1). Really? Was anyone surprised when the self-proclaimed King of Pop popped one too many doses of anesthetic?

Center while the group rehearses a few last minute changes. Senator is backstage making technical adjustments. The architectural exhibit in one room attracts my attention, but once I get beyond the first chamber, I find myself alone in a room with one other guy. Though he is probably harmless, I am not comfortable being out of earshot of Senator, so I return to the auditorium.

Sun 3:00pm~ We are fortunate to record a high quality recording of an outstanding performance of the Resonance Ensemble. They play to a packed room, as well as another hundred people sitting on the floor just outside the doors.

Sun 5:00pm~ Success! It could not have gone better. All of the equipment functioned optimally. All of the musicians were a pleasure to work with. All of the directions were accurate. Most importantly, we had a blast.

Sun 7:00pm~ Time for a well earned pizza.

Sun 7:30pm~ Time for a movie on the couch.

Sun 9:30pm~ Time for a ...zzz...zzz...zzz...

Chapter 8
Do You Know the Way to San José? How About I-5, Then?: Mid April 2011

They say the third time is a charm. When it came to taking my dream trip to the redwoods, that proved to be true. That is, it proved to be true in spite of what has come to be the traditional setbacks that precede our trips. This time, Mother Nature and the United States Government both played a role in potentially complicating our plans.

On March 11, 2011, a massive earthquake rocked Japan, sending a tsunami of epic proportions across the Pacific Ocean. Hawaii managed alright, and the West Coast of the U.S. was largely unaffected, except for a small town (pop. 4,000ish) called Crescent City. Crescent City, the destination for the bulk of our planned hiking, sustained a great deal of damage to its harbor. In Del Norte County, where we had booked an inn, the only reported U.S. death from the tsunami occurred when a man was swept out to sea while taking photographs. Out of the entire

U.S. Pacific Coast, these were the two regions that continually made the news in regard to the natural disaster.

Whether due to the tsunami or a generally rough spring, rock slides were also abundant. In fact, just a week or so before we were to check-in, a rock slide completely sealed off the only road to our inn, stranding people for several days. Again, our knack for bringing drama to otherwise pleasant vacation spots kept The Requa Inn in the headlines. (More on that later, though.)

Of course, just when the weather seemed stable, Congress did not. In somewhat necessary fights over budget cuts, the major parties faced off stubbornly, unable to settle on the long overdue numbers. The proverbial can had been kicked down the road too long, exhausting all extensions as the literal eleventh hour approached. If no agreement could be reached, the government would 'shut down' at midnight. While not as apocalyptic as it might sound, the move would close the national parks temporarily. We immediately began to plot our stealthy trespassing, in case it became necessary.

"Sir, Miss, Do you realize that this park is officially closed to the public, and as such, you are unauthorized to be here?"

"...And yet we can afford to *pay* you to patrol the area?..."

"You're going to have to step off the trail and come with me. And drop the walking stick, Miss. Sir, I'll need to confiscate your camera as well. Please be advised that any and all photos of ancient trees, rare birds, beautiful waterfalls, or blatantly stunning scenery can and will be used against you in a court of law. Now try not to enjoy your surroundings as you exit the national forest." In reality a shutdown was just barely avoided, so we did not have to get confrontational regarding our right to hike on tax-maintained public property. Either way, no one was keeping me away from my beloved big trees.

On a chilly, rainy Saturday morning, we left our home in Senator's car. We only had five days, so we booked a flight to

Portland, Oregon, and reserved a car to drive to Northern California from there. The astute reader will note that I had already broken my vow not to take Senator's car anywhere far, due to the miserable circumstances upon returning from the last trip. It shall be noted, however, that he *insisted* we put the miles on his car and leave it at the airport so that my car could stay home in the garage.

Just two miles from our house, however, the check engine light came on. He looked over at me. "You'll do anything to get your way, won't you?" he teased. We circled back into our neighborhood and switched cars, quickly cranking up the heat in Roadie.

The weather report on the television in the airport terminal showed rain and storms across the country. It continued to pour in Chicago, but at least we were in the green regions, and not the dangerous yellow or red zones. For the most part, I ignored it. We were getting wet this trip no matter what the perky blond girl said. In general, the temperature of the redwoods region stays between the low 40s and the low 60s... and it rains. You don't get 300-foot trees from sunny, dry breezes.

Though the flight was four and a half hours long (about three hours longer than I prefer), it was the smoothest flight I have ever experienced. Except for a second or two of turbulence, cruising felt like riding in a Cadillac. The landing was so clean that we almost could not feel the touchdown. Perhaps the best treat of all was that the cabin roof of our Southwest jet remained intact, unlike one of their planes that had made the news earlier in the month.

Now it was on to pick up the car. I hate renting cars, but there was no other way to do this trip in five days, so we made our first hike through many hallways, elevators, and breezeways until we finally came to the rental area. Our agency only had one couple in line ahead of us, so we figured we would be on our way quickly. Wrong. Apparently they were not going to commit to a rental agreement until they had explored every possible combination of makes, models, return dates, return times, tax rates, and probably even colors.

When they finally made their choice, we stepped up to the counter. A nice sales rep made small talk and asked us where we were going. I figured there was no harm in making polite conversation, so I explained that we were going hiking in the redwoods. Never one to miss a potential upgrade, the sales agent casually shot back, "So... you're going hiking. That means you probably want... an SUV or something about that size?"

Senator shook his head. "Nope!" I responded merrily. "Actually, I've already reserved an economy-sized car. I've already paid for it, too," I included, just to save him from having to invent his next sly query.

He was a little taken aback. "Oh, okay then. And what kind of additional insurance coverage would you like?"

"None. Thank you." He quickly explained that he just had to ask for legal purposes. "No problem." I liked this guy. He wasn't going to make any extra dough off of this sale, but I liked him nonetheless. Overall, it was probably a lame job, and he looked like he would appreciate a laugh. "So if we don't return the car next week, you'll know the bears and mountain lions got us," I casually added. Senator laughed, too, a true kindred spirit in warped humor.

We found our car, noted the various scratches and a driver's side dent on the report sheet, and drove to the exit of the garage. Here was our first encounter with a true Oregonian. I don't say they are better or worse than anybody else, but they do communicate on a different vibe.* The sixty-something gate attendant fumbled around and handed us our rental agreement

---

* More likely they are the remote, 1960s-infused cousins of the Pacific Northwest culture.

papers. "Ha yu feblubem den car sha?"

"What?" I strained my ears. He asked if we had checked for any scratches or dents. I indicated the paper I had just given him. He seemed confused, but eventually figured it out. Before he could bid us farewell, or a hearty "Later, Man", I squeezed in my question. "Can you tell me the easiest way to get to I-5?" Clearly the only major highway in the state, which connected just a few miles away from the airport, had escaped his knowledge.

"Huh?"

"Interstate 5... going south?..." Nothing. "Okay then, thanks *(for nothing)*!" Good thing we had done our map homework.

Once on I-5, we learned another handy piece of information about Oregonians. They are not comfortable speeding. They will do the speed limit (sometimes), but the moment they see the needle creep over the established mileage per hour, they pull back the reins. This is the case even if doing so means hitting the breaks in the left lane of the interstate. I kept looking for cops, thinking a driver had spotted one, but there were none.* I did not mind that they were driving slowly as much as I minded the constant awkward adjustment of trying to navigate their lane system. The drive-brake-change lanes-brake-speed up-change lanes game got old fast.

Throughout the middle of the state, our education continued. Hitchhiking is perfectly legal in Oregon. Despite the continuous rain, we saw ample evidence of this, especially when

---

* I know this for a fact because they surely would have pulled us over. Overtaking vehicles left and right at a cool 68mph would have made us a target. That is, unless the police refuse to speed, too. I haven't worked out the details of my theory yet, but I think it has something to do with keeping up the state's environmentally-friendly image. The tourists go for that sort of thing, you know.

we drove on Route 199.[*] What you may *not* do, however, is pump your own gas.

A few hours into the journey, we pulled into a gas station. As Senator was stepping out of the passenger's side to the pump, a woman came up to my driver's side window. If it had not been for her uniform shirt, I would have ignored her as a panhandler hitting up the tourists for cash. "You gettin' gas?" She asked. I nodded. *Yeah, that's the general idea.* "Fillin' up?" I nodded again, keeping an eye on her hands, just in case.

There was a dramatic pause, after which she sighed and explained. "You must be from outta' state. It's illegal to pump your own gas here. I gotta' do it." O-kaaay. That was a new one for us. Senator slid back into his seat, and I handed the woman my credit card, half wondering if I would ever see it again. Moments later the tank was full, my card was returned, and we were on our way again.

The rain continued to drive faster than most Oregonians. As if on cue, the only time the sun poked out was for the few moments we were driving through a very small town called Sunny Valley. As soon as we were through the valley, the clouds reconvened. Impressive. No false advertising there.

Soon the evening was setting in. Senator was driving stonefaced. Come to think of it, the only time he had smiled all day was when I made my stupid joke at the car rental counter. I stared at him for a moment, trying to penetrate his silent thoughts with my eyes. He was not angry or upset, but that boy was definitely preoccupied. It had been a long day that started in Illinois at dawn and would soon end in California after dusk. Once I thought about it, I recognized the mode. He was on a mission and would be fine once we reached our destination and he could relax.

---

[*] My personal favorite was a muddy couple thumbing a ride with their two muddy dogs. Good luck, guys.

We crossed the border into California, promising the bored agent that we were not harboring any illegal or undocumented produce. Soon the trees seemed to be growing bigger. Twilight made the forest even more formidable. Then, just thirty miles or so from our inn, we entered another world.

I will never forget the first moment we witnessed the magnitude of the giant California redwoods. We took yet another turn in the curvy road, but this time the view was different. We had entered the edge of a giant's woods. We both let out an audible gasp. No words or pictures can adequately describe the sheer strength and wonder that these trees pose. We were instantly reduced to specks. There are only two other times in my life where the scenery has moved me to this degree: when I saw the Grand Canyon and when I saw the Rocky Mountains for the first time. I actually swallowed a lump in my throat, while pressing my face upward against the window. The experience of being surrounded by these beautiful monsters was nothing short of spiritual.

Soon we arrived at the turnoff for our inn. The road was clearly marked with large orange square signs telling us that it was closed. Before we left home, I had read something stating that, even though the sign said the road was closed, we could still reach the inn. We drove on. After all, we had no other alternatives.

About a mile down the road there was a stop sign. There was no intersection, but there was a mound of rock that had been pushed just far enough off of the road to supply one unobstructed lane. It read, "Watch for falling rock. Then proceed with caution." Believe me, we did. Fortunately, none of the slide remnants befell us, and we turned safely into the parking lot of our inn.

The Requa Inn is clean, comfortable, charming, and lovely, which is especially convenient because it is just about the only non-RV park around. Serving as an inn since 1914, the

Requa has no phones, televisions, or clocks in the guest rooms. That is not to say it is primitive; there was plenty of space, a great bed, and an ample bathroom. Don't rely too heavily on your cell phone or an internet connection, though; both receive weak signals on a good day. For this alone they earned bonus points with us.

We checked in, helped ourselves to coffee, and settled into bed among a pile of maps and brochures. I could not wait to see, touch, and smell the forest up close. I looked over at Senator. For the first time since leaving home he looked content and genuinely pleased. The tense expression had left his face, and he had given himself permission to forget about work, forget about the studio, and relax as the Klamath River quietly floated past our window.

After a night of random dreams about trees, I woke up way too early. I was tired, but excited. It had rained faithfully through the night and showed no sign of letting up, but we were here, so we might as well get used to the idea of getting wet. After a homemade breakfast in the inn's dining room, we set out for our first expedition.

The Yurok Trail climbed up along an inlet of the coast. The plants were vibrantly green, but the beach below was a charcoal plane with huge trunks of black driftwood scattered all along the inside edge. The ocean horizon was lost in a sea of gray mist, but it was in no way drab. Birds called from several directions, and the waves pounded out their soothing music against the rocks. This was not the California coast I had expected. It reminded me more of photos of the northwest coast of Great Britain.

Within five minutes my feet were soaked. Thankfully, it was not cold, but I had to do my best to ignore the ever-present *squish*. Senator's shoes were somewhat better, but the bottom few inches of his jeans were drenched like mine. At some point, the footwear situation would have to be reassessed.

Our next stop was Jedediah Smith State Park. A park ranger had suggested we try the Boy Scout Trail. While the name conjured up images of hoards of nine-year olds sloshing about loudly, slapping each other with fern fronds and giggling over who could pee the furthest in the woods, I decided to trust him. We drove an unpaved, significantly potholed road to the trailhead. Reader, if you only make it to the redwoods once in your life, go to this state park. If you only make it to this park once in your life, hike this trail.

From the very first step you are surrounded by some of the park's tallest and widest trees. On the day we hiked, the mist gave an eerie depth to the various layers of the forest, adding to its natural beauty. Covering the forest floor, supersized ferns and many other overgrown species add to the Jurassic Park effect. Humans look downright silly against the massive scale.

Miraculously, everything was larger except the bugs. In fact, despite the drizzly weather, we did not encounter a single mosquito. Hiking the redwoods was what I imagined hiking an exotic rainforest to be, minus the 300-pound snakes, poisonous plants, and man-and-woman-eating beasts. In short, it was a soggy paradise.

After a few miles on Boyscout Trail, we decided to try another hike. We got back into the car, cranked the heat (which produced more steam than dry air), and nibbled some crackers. Like dummies, we had forgotten our water, so we remedied the situation by eating salt. Somehow, amid the magic of vacation, these types of less-than-genius moves work. At home, we would probably be sick from dehydration.

Stout Grove was another trail recommended by the ranger. I have to admit, I was again skeptical at first. It was one of those trails that was widely marked, well maintained, uninterestingly level, and suitable for ages 2-92. In short, it was the ideal trail for someone who wanted to claim technical bragging rights at having conquered the redwoods. I kept these thoughts to myself as we stepped out of the car into the steady drizzle. A few relatively dry children scampered back from the path. Apparently their hike was not long enough for the rain to soak them, and not strenuous enough to break a sweat.

Upon actually experiencing Stout Grove, my opinion of it changed significantly. The unique feature of this particular area in the woods is the many fallen redwoods. Seeing them horizontally gives yet another perspective of their scope. Reclining giants form playhouse-sized nooks and hollows, perfect for exploring or hiding within. As the trees decompose, the nutrient-dense nurseries provide the forest with the next generation of baby giants.

Naturally, we had left the camera in the car. Choosing just to enjoy the moment and memory privately, sans documentation, we held hands as we meandered slowly along the trail. Not that the pictures have done justice to any of the trip. Senator put it best when he declared that he had never seen so many shades of green. I smiled at the senior citizen couple who had paused to inspect one of the trees. I guess sometimes a short, easy trail is necessary. I breathed in deeply as we sloshed our way back to the parking lot.

And slosh we did. I think my feet have been drier in the shower. There was no way these shoes would be dry in time for more hiking the next day. *Had I seen a Payless on the way through town?*

We consulted the map to find our last trailhead of the day. The road took us over and along a rushing river. On the other side was a rustic neighborhood with lovely views of the water and the park. Several miles downstream, this river spilled into the Pacific Ocean, which Senator observed, begs the question: how do the freshwater fish know when to stop? Do they just swim along in blissful ignorance until suddenly their eyes start burning, and their gills sputter as they choke out the salty water? When they realize that all of their schoolmates are experiencing the same unpleasant sensation, do they blame the guy at the head of the class? Somebody somewhere took a wrong turn...

As maps and other natural wonders would have it, we never did find parking for access to the last trail. We did find ourselves getting tired, though. We had hiked several miles on foot already that day, so we agreed to skip the last trail and head back into town. After all, we had already tempted fate by going too long without water. The ironic objective became 1.)obtaining water for our parched insides, and 2.)obtaining dry shoes for our drenched outsides.

At times I experience minor psychic or foreshadowing moments, which generally turn out to be useless, as my friends will testify. Randomly noticing a Payless shoe store on the way into town though, was nothing short of divine revelation. I still did not have much hope that I would find any hiking boots. The average nine-year old (whose size I generally wear,) does not usually have need of durable footwear, hence my lame tennis shoes. Senator and I stepped into the store, acknowledged the slightly curious look of the sales clerk, and separated toward our respective departments-- he to men's and I to kids'.

Then, joy of joys, a ray of light shone down and illuminated a box containing high top, waterproof hiking boots in my exact size. Or something to that effect. I couldn't believe my fortune as I tried to look casual while wrestling my wet socks off to try on the boots. A perfect fit! The new boots were 100% man made materials, which was a considerable upgrade from my current shoes, which were 50% man made materials and 50% natural mud, leaves, and pine needles. I imagined the luxury of hiking with dry feet the next day. Some girls dream of dancing in glass slippers with their princes; I just wanted to hike in dry boots with mine. When Senator had found a suitable pair for himself, we paid for our vacation souvenirs and headed to the grocery store to stock up on water.

Just a few miles before returning to our inn, we stopped off at the End of the Trail Museum. While the museum sits on the property of a tacky tourist trap,* it is an excellent private collection of Native American artifacts. The free exhibit spans four or five rooms, each devoted to a different section of North America. Baskets, jewelry, clothing, tools, weapons, paintings, and personal belongings tell the story of the laborious daily life and the complex social changes that faced the first Americans. Hundred-year old postcards added the transplanted Europeans' perspective. It was good to understand the history of the land and the people of a region. In some respect, traveling is incomplete without this kind of background education.

We concluded our tour of the museum and walked out to the car. We began to realize just how tired we were. Thankfully, the inn was less than ten minutes away. We just had to figure out how to get to our room without tracking in too much mud.

After carefully placing our mud sculptures on plastic bags next to the heater, we cleaned up and spent some time relaxing. The mist still hung over the river, not in too much of a hurry to do anything. We could relate. Fortunately, the only things on the evening's agenda were dinner and doing more nothing.

Actually, I should qualify the "nothing" by explaining that nothing of exertion took place. The inn's living room looked so inviting that we decided to stay downstairs for the evening to read. Then, for reasons yet unclear, I became mildly obsessed with the idea of doing a jigsaw puzzle. This was partly in defiance to prove to myself that I was on vacation. At home, a few puzzles sit unloved in a hall closet, prioritized far below

---

* In addition to viewing the multi-story Paul Bunyan and Babe statues, you can dine at a café under a canopy of plastic flowers, or under a ceiling painted to look like a river surface, complete with the lower half of ducks hovering about you.

jobs, housework, writing, family, friends, and life. Here, 500 pieces called out to me. I *had* to unite them to bring the generic birdhouse scene to life.

Senator put down his book and started to help me sort edges from middle pieces. We worked silently for a while, until he confirmed my suspicions. "Baby, I don't think all of the pieces are here." Of course he was right. When was the last time any used puzzle had every piece? I valiantly plowed through for another half hour or so, connecting islands of pieces that would never realize their full continental potential. Senator smiled at my futile determination. The real entertainment was in the people watching, anyway.

On that particular night, six or seven rooms were booked at the inn. Most of them were reserved by average inngoers like ourselves. Two parties, however, caught our attention. First, there was Panic Girl. As we shuffled puzzle pieces around aimlessly, we became aware of a woman who was upset at having lost something. Her companion helped her look, but nothing was turning up. We assumed that she had misplaced her purse, or perhaps a credit card. She was becoming frantic. I felt bad for her. Everyone at some point has known that horrible, sick feeling. Not wanting to but in, we quietly glanced around our surroundings, but there was nothing to report.

Then we overheard the crucial details. As it turned out, the treasure in question was a stupid $4 map. *Are you kidding me?* I was glad we had not offered to help out loud. The couple looked to be in their mid-20s, and all we could think was, boy is this guy in for a high maintenance and potentially psychotic ride.

The great room settled down once again, allowing us to overhear the second group of interest. The Enlightened Family consisted of a soft spoken man of undetermined sexual preference, a middle-aged woman who seemed to be toying with the Mommy role while making sure to mention her environmentalist career at opportune moments, and a six-year old who was not about to give up her baby pacifier. The three of them played Monopoly in decidedly NPR* voices, all the while careful not to embrace capitalism *too* enthusiastically. Occasionally the little girl mumbled questions or made observations, safely tucked behind her binky. Did anyone else think this was just a bit odd?! As they waited for the child's ruling as to which parent should clean up the game, and which parent should tuck her in, we took our cue and went to our room.

I do not remember much about falling asleep, but I was awake early again the next morning. I was just as tired as the day before, but also just as excited about the four shorter trails we were planning to hike. Our new, dry boots stood ready by the door. As I waited for Senator to wake up, I reviewed the maps for Prairie Creek State Park one more time.

At breakfast we noticed that the river and the sky looked different. The mist was not as thick, the water was moving slowly, and there was a sort of yellowish bright light in the sky. Come to think of it, behind the yellowish thing was a field of blue. It had stopped raining for the first time since we had left Chicago.

We eagerly set out for trail number one. Supposedly the trail led to a meadow where elk frequently roamed. Just after we took the appropriate exit, however, we learned that the road was closed due to flooding. Instead, a side road led us to another trail.

The new trail was unmarked, but by my estimation it would either link up with the desired trail, or lead us down to an ocean beach. Either one would have been acceptable. Neither one occurred. The new trail, (which put our new footwear to the test as it was 90% covered in flowing streams,) switched back and forth narrowly down the hill. The trees were not as big, but

---

* National Public Radio.... ssshhhhh!

the plants were lush and vibrant. Eventually we turned a bend that led to a steep ridge with a view of a wide creek. That was it. The strenuous trail fizzled to a dead end at a mud slide about a mile in. There was nothing left to do here except hustle back up the hill. On to the next hike.

The road for the second trail was also closed because of a mud slide. This time there were no 'mystery trail' options around, so we left that end of the park. The great thing about Prairie Creek is that there are many acres of back country. This keeps it relatively unspoiled. The drawback to such purity is that there are very few roads in or out of the park. We were now down to about 50% of the original access to the park, but we could still try the southern route.

Trail number three was a success, at least as far as the parking lot. As we turned into the entrance, we even saw a lazy herd of elk, who were people watching. We parked and noticed that the road beyond the parking lot was closed. This time, no reason was posted. Who cares? Make one up.

Somewhere in the vicinity, brochures and visitor guides boasted the existence of the unoriginally named Big Tree. Several trails converged, so we picked the one that led in the general direction of B.T.. The walk was easy, and the woods were sparse enough to give the impression that you were watching a play with multiple scene layers unfolding. The forest gave off that intense earthy-clean smell that I find intoxicating and romantic. I held Senator's hand and we walked down the trail. "Oh good-- a sign."

I dropped Senator's hand and my shoulders sagged. The marker for Big Tree read "1 mile", but pointed in the exact opposite direction of which we were walking. I felt like an idiot, especially as Senator has build up this legend in his mind of my extraordinary directional sense. Undeterred, we did a 180° and continued along the beautiful trail.

Fifteen minutes later, it still felt wrong. Senator thought

so too, rebuilding my confidence. "Now wait a minute. This doesn't even make sense. Everything else is in place, but the loop we want should be north of here. Is it possible that a permanent sign could be completely wrong?"

"It could be permanently wrong," answered Senator. I was vindicated. I asked him if he would be willing to try one more strategy with me. Enjoying the whole experience of the forest, he nodded in agreement. Once again we altered our direction. This time we walked on the paved road that had been closed to cars.

Sure enough, at about one mile in, we saw the big sign for Big Tree. Before taking the equally obviously named Circle Trail to the elusive Big Tree, we read the posted warning sign. Menacing geometric illustrations and a bevy of cautions made it seem like we would be lucky to get out without fighting a bear or mountain lion. The sign suggested we talk or make noise to announce our presence to any unsuspecting bears. "...SO I GUESS WE SHOULD STARTING TALKING LOUDLY....," I began, with a nerdy giggle. Just then a woman walked out from the woods, surprising me enough to make me jump, which in turn made Senator jump when I squeezed his hand hard. She glanced at us questioningly for a second as she went by. If she wasn't annoyed by tourists before, she probably was now.

As it turned out, the famous Big Tree *was* big. In fact, at 1,500 years old, it was quite big. It was not the biggest tree we had seen during the previous twenty-four hours, though. "Eh," said Senator, as he shrugged his opinion. It was amazing how quickly we had become spoiled by the giants. We surveyed the girth of the trunk, joined hands again, and walked back down the trail. This time, we threw caution to the wind and spoke in soft voices, mountain lions notwithstanding.

The last proposed trail of the day would have taken us to Fern Canyon. As you have probably guessed by now, it boasted a stunning canyon with larger-than-life ferns. Or so we are told.

Yet another road was closed due to flooding. This time the washed out area was right at the gate, which provided a good fifteen minutes of cheap entertainment as we watched drivers decide whether or not to chance it. A couple of them made it through, but we could see that the water level was above the door seam. That would be a hard one to explain to the rental agency.*

All told, we actually did hike several miles, which was impressive considering about 90% of the park was inaccessible. We voted it satisfactory, and set out onto the main highway. Forests, valleys, and the coast were all visible along Highway 101. Just then I noticed a sign for Bald Hills Road.

"I don't remember the details, but something somewhere said it was a good scenic drive to take," I blurted out. Senator exited to a road that climbed steeply. As we wound around the hills, in and out of the mist, it was never clear whether we were on a state road, private property, or national park territory. Since no one came out with shotguns, we kept going.

We came to a short turnoff and stopped the car. We had ascended further than we realized. Looking out across the panorama yielded a stunning view. In the distance were twin hills whose tops were bare. Further down the hills, the tree line started, continuing densely to the bottom. Below, a lush valley of yet another shade of green sprawled out around a dried up riverbed. Hawks caught the unobstructed breezes overhead. It was an idyllic scene, but I will always prefer the misty mystery of the redwood forest on a drizzly day.

Alright, enough with the schmaltz and on to the kitsch. There was a time in our naïve U.S. history when we believed that all of the earth's treasures existed for commercial entertainment purposes. While this will always be true to some degree, we no longer encourage the destruction of such wonders to that end.

---

*   especially since they only spoke Oregonian

As the cartoons of yore clearly depict, however, remnants of that era do exist, in all of their cheesy glory.

When you tell someone that you are going to the redwoods, two comments usually follow. People feel compelled to acknowledge that those are some big trees, yesiree. Then a light bulb goes on, they reach back into their knowledge of pop culture and early 20th century travel, and they retrieve a picture of a carved out tree. "Hey, isn't there a tree you can *drive* through out there?! You should do that!"

Indeed there is and indeed we should. The Tour Thru Tree is located on the Yurok reservation in Klamath, California. While natives of old had trouble comprehending land ownership, that no longer seemed to be a hindrance. Touring "thru" this redwood will cost you five bucks. If no one is in the toll booth, just drop your money in the box.

"You got a five?" asked Senator, amused by the entrepreneurial situation.

"Heck yeah!" I handed over the fin and we drove up a hill to the famous butchered tree, which had sacrificed the better part of its most recent century to the tourism industry.

Coincidentally, a white car of the same make and model as our rental was creeping through the tree carefully as we pulled up. They made it fine, but when we tried, it was a little too close for comfort. Senator backed the car out. We instead chose to tour thru on foot.

Senator set the timer on the camera as we stood within the trunk of the dripping tree. It had never occurred to me that trees were so wet inside, but it made sense. Water was the lifeline of the tree, and for something that tall to live, it had to have an efficient delivery system. Lost in my thoughts, I did not notice that Senator was in prime position to flip me upside down and spin me around. I screamed and choked on laughter. All I could see was a chaotic flash of redwood before he put me down in my unsteady dizziness. Good tour thru.

We left the Tour Thru Tree and headed back toward our inn. At the time, we were too tired to backtrack, but in retrospect, I wish we would have taken an hour to view another local curiosity. Among the gentle slopes by the coast is what appears to be an average working farm. In reality, it is a disguised World War II radar station. With so much uncertainty in the Pacific, the station was established to help guard the West Coast against potential air threats from the Japanese. Trinidad Radar Station, (also known as Radar Station B-71) remained operational throughout the war and was eventually acquired by the National Park Service.* If you get there before me, Reader, write me and tell me if it's as cool as it sounds.

We arrived back at the inn mid-afternoon. There was plenty of time before dinner, so we decided to continue past the inn, up the road in the other direction. Since the inn sat along the river that emptied into the ocean, I hoped there would be some good views at the end of the road. We were not disappointed.

After slowly climbing in elevation for about two miles, there was a small parking lot turnoff. There, the continent ended, and the largest ocean on Earth began. The low tide exposed a wide, flat, grayish-chocolate colored sand bar. Waves slapped boulders close to shore, while further out it was harder to distinguish what was going on. We pulled out the binoculars for a closer look. Either something was rising out of the water, or the water was dipping beneath something. It was too difficult to tell.

After watching certain spots for a while with no change in movement, we concluded that we had been faithfully tracking migrating rocks. In one instance, however, we both believe we saw the markings of a killer whale in the distance. Furthermore, the object in question changed its position within our field of

---

* See www.militarymuseum.org/KlamathRadarStn for more information.

view. After an officially summoned impromptu family meeting, it was declared a killer whale (*Orcinus orca*). This turned out to be a grand moment as, despite attending the many places where we *should* have spotted whales according to multiple available literature, we saw no other mammals of the deep for the remainder of the trip.

When we had our fill (yeah right) of sunny, serene panoramic vistas, we returned to the inn. After dropping our things off, we strolled across the street to the riverfront. Somebody at some point in time had recognized it as an ideal place to perch a glider swing, so we indulged. For a while we talked, and for a while we were silent. I was amazed at all we had taken in during the past two days. I was amazed at all we had taken in during the past eight years. I was amazed that my feet were still dry after hiking for hours....

Dinner was the same pasta dish as the previous night. It was tasty, but we couldn't help thinking that it was the staple just-in-case-vegetarians-show-up dish. I suspected that if we ate there another night, we would have become quite the experts on the entrée. We regularly prepare more exciting pasta dishes at home, but the food was never the point of the trip. We were alone together, separated from our work by over 2,000 miles. "Remind me again why I only planned two days to explore these woods..." I mused.

The night concluded peacefully. No one at the inn suffered the anxiety that only a lost map can conjure. No one fretted the sociopolitical implications of board games. Senator read his mystery classic. I read about where we had gone and where we were going the next day, drinking in every detail.

The next morning the sky was still mostly clear. Everyone seemed excited by the prospect of two sunny days in a row. While I looked forward to more great ocean views, I actually missed the mist.* Nothing can replace the shrouded romance of a thinly veiled forest, where fog hangs like ghosts waiting to tell their stories.

There would be no more ghosts on this trip, however. We sat down to breakfast as I adjusted my chair to look directly at Senator, instead of directly into the sun. The spread before us contained pancakes, yogurt, granola, toast, fruit, juice, and coffee. Senator indulged because it would be a long time before we would eat again. I indulged because I had made the mistake of ordering pancakes the previous morning, without first checking on the flavor du jour. Many great ingredients can nestle deliciously within the folds of hot cakes, but poppy seed is not one of them. This time, I was taking no chances.

After breakfast, we checked out and drove twenty miles to an overlook where we were almost certainly guaranteed to see whales and/or sea lions. (But you already know how that turned out.) Unfazed, we continued north on Highway 101. Whereas we were rushed on the way down from Portland, we had much more leisure time on the drive back.

This scenic drives has to rank in the top ten in our beautiful country. To the east stand rolling hills covered with dense, tall forest. While most of the trees are not redwoods, the pines are staggering. To the west is the ocean, and due to expert planning, most of the view is unobstructed. You could conceivably spend hours watching the ocean without ever stopping your car. The water changes tones here, too. More green is added, and when the sun hits it just right, the surface glows like a field of gems. Too poetic? Don't knock it until you have seen it.

State parks line almost the entire Oregon coast. It could really be one giant national seashore; there are not many gaps for private land. That is not to say that it is boring, however. Just

---

* Ain't homophones grand?

when you think it is all the same, the terrain changes. The trees near the shoreline disappear, replaced by giant sand dunes. For the next hour or so, it feels like you are driving next to a Hollywood backdrop from a movie set in the Sahara.

In my determination to stay well hydrated, I drank plenty of water and coffee, which meant a pit stop was soon necessary. We pulled into a gas station, remembering to let the attendant pump the verboten fuel. I stepped out in search of a restroom. The only accommodation was a one room john on the outside of the building. I stepped inside and carefully bolted the lock.

Thankfully I was finished with the essentials as the door flew open. A burst of afternoon sunlight and one very embarrassed guy-- about my age-- entered my view. He was overly apologetic, but neither of us had known the lock was broken. *Well, there you are.* I had seen Oregon and Oregon had seen me. No use sweating it.

Perhaps the funniest part of the drive back to Portland was our jaunt through The Safety Corridor. There, in the middle of farmland and not much else, was a reserved twenty mile section of highway, where danger dare not lurk. Completely random signs encouraged temporarily deputized motorists to drive with their lights on, wear seatbelts, observe the speed limit (55mph), and avoid any and all distractions. Phoning, texting, makeuping, radio changing, and other such daring activities had no place here, thank you very much. Then, just as abruptly as it began, The Safety Corridor ended. Woo-hoo! I halfway expected people to floor it while changing lanes haphazardly between texting and knocking back a cold one, slaves to safety no more!

I have two theories on the existence of The Safety Corridor. Number one is that it is just a front for The Revenue Corridor. As it was not in any city's limits, maybe local police take turns monitoring it for opportunities to ticket the unsafe. Theory the second proposes that a dirty politician needed some image polishing. By slapping up a few signs and designating the secure zone, he/she could appear caring and cautious to the public. I am, of course, open to outside theories and proposals.

By evening we were in Portland. Rush hour traffic on a week night went far in dispelling my illusions of a green and blossoming city of pedestrians and cyclists. This just felt like Chicago with smaller buildings. According to the radio, most routes that we did not need to take were perfectly clear. Somewhere ahead on our road though, there was an accident.

Then there was the search for a hotel. I had assumed we would find a quiet inn or bed and breakfast, but those must have all been kept neatly tucked away. We bypassed one exit that featured the standard chain hotels and motels and crossed the river into Washington. Downtown Vancouver was congested and not very well laid out, so we found ourselves crossing back into Oregon. Senator and I were both frustrated. Finally, we pulled into the first decent looking place we saw.

It was right by the airport, which would be a plus in the morning. When we went inside, however, I was a little concerned that it would be out of our price range. Senator said he did not care, and he just wanted to settle in and find something to eat. He checked in and we took the elevator to the fifth floor.

When we entered our room, we realized that we had, in fact, booked a suite for the night.* The very stylish living room had a large hi-def television. So did the bedroom, just in case we decided to forgo any pleasantries in favor of not speaking to each other the rest of the night.

The kitchenette was convenient, but we had nothing to cook. Most importantly, the shower was hot and the pillows

---

* Anytime you walk in the door of your room and you can't see the bed, you know you are somewhere beyond the local Best Western. Either that, or you have erroneously walked into someone's home, in which case, you should excuse yourself politely and hasten your exit.

were soft. All we needed was a bite to eat. On that note, why does driving all day make a body so hungry? It is not as though one is burning many calories. Adjusting the blinker and flexing on the accelerator can't be that strenuous.

We drove up the road a few blocks. We agreed not to be picky. At this point, anything that was not called Jim Bob's House O' Dead Critters was fair game. I perked up. "Hey, does that sign say what I think it says?" I asked Senator.

"Nice! This is the place, V." He pulled into the parking lot of the Indian buffet. Inside we were warmly greeted, quickly sat, and easily directed to the feast of choices. We downed our fill of veggies and curry sauces and those delicious fried spinach things that would be considered unhealthy junk food in any other setting. We were satisfied and grateful. It was one of the those amazing moments that worked out exactly as it should have. All that remained of the evening was heading back to the hotel and falling asleep between Senator and Mount Hood.*

A later flight the next morning left us time to get ready and have breakfast. We had already filled up-- that is, let an attendant fill up-- the rental car, so we drove directly to the return garage. Just four days had passed since we rented the car, but I had forgotten how clueless the company's employees were. The attendant slid into the driver's seat, made some notes on his clipboard, and then handed me a bill for $18 for 'fuel service'.

I did some quick math, determined that driving six blocks did not burn up $18 worth of gas (no matter how bad prices were), and decided that patience had no place here. "What's this?" I snapped.

"Oh, the tank's not full," he answered matter-of-factly.

---

* The mountain is stunning on the eastern horizon. Unfortunately, Portlandians do not get to see it much during the cooler months. We were told that the night we were in town was the first time the mount had been visible in two months.

162

The idiot gave this ludicrous explanation as the needle on the gas gauge stayed firmly planted on 'full'. Now I was ticked.

"No. We just filled up a mile away from here, and if your car used that much gas, you have a hole in the tank. Take this off of my bill NOW." What did I have to lose? Senator backed me up, but the well-trained scammer referred us to the woman at the agency's counter. I repeated my claim to her, just as directly, but in a more subdued manner, as she had not yet accused us of not filling up.

Then she started in. "Where did you fill up?"

"I don't remember the name of the place, but it's right down the street from Embassy Suites." *Give me a break!* She just lost her polite-version-of-the-complaint privileges.

"Hhmmm," she muttered, doing her best Church Lady impersonation while looking down at her screen and down at us. "I don't remember seeing a gas station by there."

"Look, it's right on 82nd Street. Do you want to see the receipt?!" I gave her my best wide-eyed look of incredulity-- the one I have used on students on necessary occasions.

"No.... that's okay," she sighed under protest. Truly she was put out. "I'll take it off your bill," she relented.

"Thank you." I signed the new receipt and we left. Did I overreact? Senator didn't think so, but I'm sure the entire staff at the car rental agency thought so. You see, Reader, I hate deception in any form, from major lying and cheating to bogus $18 charges that someone hopes I'm too stupid to notice or too weak to contradict. I guess this is one of the many reasons I am with Senator. In eight years we have had very few arguments, but they have all been upfront. If you do not have honesty, you do not have anything.

Thankfully, check-in and security were a breeze, so we found ourselves at our terminal with more than an hour to spare. I guess the fight for justice had given us an appetite because we were both tempted by the Mexican restaurant in the airport. It would be a long time until we were home, so we sat down and picked up menus. I was surprised at the moderate prices. I was even more surprised when the food arrived, garden-fresh and authentically prepared. I had expected it to be more of a glorified Taco Bell. Portland-- a city of great restaurants, even in their airport.

We relaxed a while before boarding our flight. The plane was full again, but we were comfortable, and the afternoon flight turned into a sunset flight as we moved across time zones. Remembering the last miserable trip home from New York, I thanked God that we were both feeling well. Soon Senator was dozing, puffing his lips out in his characteristic way when he exhaled. The pilot's voice on the intercom interrupted my thoughts. "Ladies and Gentlemen, we should be arriving in Chicago about twenty minutes early, under sunny skies. Enjoy the rest of your flight."

Afterword

Forty-nine down and one to go-- not that I am keeping track or anything. It will be a few more years before we make it to the land of leis and luaus, but considering how busy life had become during the two years in which this book takes place, it is amazing that we made it anywhere other than Chicago. Senator had been recording experimental jazz artists for two yeas, and he had earned enough of a positive reputation to keep him active in the studio, while still maintaining his full time job.

That either of us had/have jobs during the worst recession of our lifetime is surprising. Grateful for employment, I continued to teach and edit. Not often enough, I wrote. Then I decided it would be exciting to take on a more active role in the business and roadie end of the studio. (It was, and is, an ever-evolving fun, inspiring, sleep-depriving challenge.)

In life, few people have time and money simultaneously. During some periods we had more money than in others, but we never had enough time. Thank God we never sat around waiting for spare weeks, days, or moments to experience life, lands, and love. And now I'll conclude, because I could really use a nap, but...

~Wendy V
May 2011

www.ingramcontent.com/pod-product-compliance
Lightning Source LLC
LaVergne TN
LVHW041623070426
835507LV00008B/415